Coloring
Locals

Coloring Locals

Racial Formation
in Kate Chopin's
Youth's Companion
Stories

Bonnie James Shaker

University of Iowa Press

Iowa City

University of Iowa Press,
Iowa City 52242
Copyright © 2003 by the
University of Iowa Press

Design by Richard Hendel
http://www.uiowa.edu/uiowapress

Youth's Companion illustrations produced
by ProQuest Information and Learning
Company. Inquiries may be made to:
ProQuest Information and Learning
Company, 300 North Zeeb Road,
Ann Arbor, MI 48106-1346 USA.
Telephone (734) 761-7400;
e-mail: info@il.proquest.com;
Web page: www.il.proquest.com.

An early version of chapter 2 was
published as " 'Lookin' Jis' like W'ite Folks':
Coloring Locals in Kate Chopin's 'A Rude
Awakening' " in *Louisiana Literature*
14.2 (Fall 1997): 116–25.

Letters of William Henry Rideing
to William Morris Colles. Boston Public
Library/Rare Books Department.
Reprinted courtesy of the Trustees.

The publication of this book was
generously supported by the University
of Iowa Foundation.

Printed on acid-free paper

Library of Congress
Cataloging-in-Publication Data

Shaker, Bonnie James, 1960–
Coloring locals: racial formation in Kate
Chopin's Youth's Companion stories/
Bonnie James Shaker.
p.   cm.
Includes bibliographical references (p.   )
and index.
ISBN 0-87745-828-6 (cloth)
1. Chopin, Kate, 1851–1904 — Criticism and
interpretation.   2. Women and literature
—Louisiana—History—19th century.
3. Chopin, Kate, 1851–1904—Views on
race.   4. Louisiana—In literature.
5. Local color in literature.   6. Racism in
literature.   7. Race in literature.   I. Title.
PS1294.C63 S48 2003
813'.4—dc21   2002021764

03   04   05   06   07   C   5   4   3   2   1

For Erma and Bill, who made things possible then;
for Chris and Dana, who make things possible now;
and for young Billy, my greatest childhood fan.

CONTENTS

ACKNOWLEDGMENTS

Writing this book made me feel more like Edna Pontellier than was comfortable.

Even at the turn of the twenty-first century, it is difficult for a woman to extricate herself from maternal and marital obligations. Today as in the past, all members of the family unit must do their part in order to keep the organism running. Fourth-grade science homework does not wait for the editing of a chapter, nor do potatoes hop into boiling water on their own in preparation for a healthful home-cooked meal.

But thankfully I am not one of my nineteenth-century sisters, fictional or historical. In the twenty-first century, familial roles are more flexible, and both immediate and extended family may be reasoned with to wait until "after the book." Daughters, even in the fourth grade, can be taken into their mothers' confidences to ease the double bind of work and family, and husbands do wash clothes and bring home dinner in support of their wives' professional ambitions.

Clearly, this book is a collaboration of many efforts. I am therefore indebted to the following:

First and foremost, the editors at the University of Iowa Press, for their infinite patience and support of this project.

The members of my dissertation committee at Case Western Reserve University, Suzanne Ferguson, Judith Oster, Roger Salomon, and Angela Woollacott, for their contributions to this book in its embryonic form.

The Armington Research Program on Values in Children at CWRU, for the generous grant that enabled my travel first to Boston to study the Rideing letters and view Chopin's texts as they appeared in the original, folio-sized *Youth's Companion* issues held in the Rare Books and Manuscripts Room of the Boston Public Library, and then to St. Louis to review Chopin's private papers at the Missouri Historical Society. My thanks also to the able and accommodating librarians at both repositories.

The staff of the William F. Maag Jr. Library at Youngstown State University, especially Thomas Atwood and Jean Romeo and, in the Microforms Center, Ellen Banks and Bob Ault.

Those teachers who helped me shape an enduring sense of myself as a writer, a scholar, and a feminist: Judy Barron, Lila Hanft, Vivetta Petronio, Sally Robinson, and again, Roger Salomon.

My co-workers at Youngstown State University, among them Sherry Linkon, Bill Mullen, and Gary Salvner — who remain everyone's idea of ideal colleagues — and the students there who have taught me so much, especially Patrecka Adams, Jahi Harvey, and Larissa Theodore.

Each of those women who have furthered my scholarship through suggestions, conversations, professional mentoring, personal friendship, or all of the above: Young Duck Chung, Angie Gianoglio, Mary Giffin, Sandra Gunning, Ann Marie Hebert, Amy Kesegich, Kirsten Leonard, Lisa Maruca, Karen McBride Sekanick, Sherri Tenpenny, Roberta Seelinger Trites, Sarah Turner, and Stephanie Wiery.

And earlier generations of Mumaws and Jameses, who taught me discipline and gave me love.

Kate Chopin's canonical status as a feminist rebel and broad social reformer conflicts with the fact that one of the most supportive publishers throughout her lifetime was the *Youth's Companion*, a juvenile periodical whose self-promotion as a product "for all the family" contributed to its success as the longest-running and, at one time, most widely circulating periodical in nineteenth-century America. The *Companion*, a little-discussed component of the Chopin oeuvre, supported her work from the beginning to the very end of her career and provided Chopin with her single largest source of literary income. This seemingly contradictory fact — that the daring author of *The Awakening* found a welcoming forum for much of her work in one of the century's greatest "family values" periodicals — has yet to be addressed.[1]

Contrary to the fiction for which she is best known, Chopin's *Companion* tales frequently embrace orthodox notions of femininity and, notably, masculinity as well. Although an uncomplicated explanation for this phenomenon is that Chopin wrote her fiction with an eye toward the periodical's sense of propriety — which she did — she was not simply forsaking her feminist politics for editorial acceptance. With few exceptions, Chopin's endorsement of conventional gender norms in her *Companion* stories, 1891–1902, operates in the service of a critical agenda beyond her feminism, one that has yet to be identified as such, and one that can help us appreciate nuances of identity construction previously misunderstood or overlooked in the body of her work.

This agenda I articulate as the discursive act of coloring locals, or the narrative construction of racial difference for Louisiana peoples of African American, Native American, and French and Spanish American ancestries. Because the proliferative periodical industry of the Gilded Age was constructing a truly national audience for the first time in American history and because regional literature was mediating for those masses the complex foreign-born and native-born heritages of the country's particular locales, the local color fiction movement, in which Chopin's writing is situated, participated squarely within what the Nineteenth-Century

American Women Writers' Group has called the "race for race,"[2] or the competitive game of articulating racial difference for a diverse post-Reconstruction population that included freed people, first-generation free-born African Americans, Catholic European Americans, Jewish Americans, and immigrants from around the globe. I am interested in mapping that race for race throughout Chopin's fiction, and I argue that what she was rushing to achieve was the designation of whiteness for specific groups of people, a designation that conferred not only social preferment but also civil protections and political enfranchisement.

For Chopin, "coloring locals" meant transforming non-Louisianians' general understanding of the Creole and Cajun as mixed-race people into "purely" white folks.[3] Like her other fiction, Chopin's *Companion* tales overwhelmingly figure Creoles as the descendants of exclusively white French aristocracy and, metaphorically speaking, Cajuns as their "country cousins," reserving racial otherness for African Americans and Native Americans.[4] Thus, we can explain why, when Chopin is concerned with coloring Creoles and Cajuns white, she strategically deploys notions of genteel femininity and masculinity for the advantages they afford as signs of Creole and Cajun respectability and hence white racial assimilation. She does not permit her *Companion* Creole and Cajun characters gender transgressions, except to teach them the error of their ways. Nor does she critique gender ideology in these texts, as she does in so many short stories published outside the *Companion* featuring Creole and American characters already culturally intelligible as white.

Such a critical re-visioning of Chopin's life and work requires privileging information Chopin scholarship has long acknowledged but subordinated: namely, that she gained her national reputation first and foremost as a writer of short fiction for juvenile periodicals. Between 1891 and 1902 Chopin successfully placed one story in *Wide Awake*, four in *Harper's Young People*, and eleven in the *Youth's Companion*. She earned $787 from these magazines, a sum that equals more than one-third of her lifetime's $2300 literary income.

Chopin had a longer relationship with the *Companion* than with any other periodical. She published her first *Companion* story, "For Marse Chouchoute," only twenty months after she debuted "Wiser Than a God" in the *Philadelphia Musical Journal* in December 1889, and her last two, "The Wood-Choppers" and "Polly," in 1902, just two years before she died. Although it did not print all of the twenty short stories it bought from her, the *Companion* paid Chopin $750 in all, her largest income from a single publisher.

Chopin had ample incentive besides income to privilege her conservative racial agenda over her feminism for the *Companion*. In the 1890s, when Chopin was writing and marketing her fiction, the *Companion* could offer new writers — especially women — unprecedented visibility. With the exception of mail-order papers, the *Companion* outpaced all other American magazines in 1885 with a circulation of 385,000; in 1890, with a circulation of one-half million, it fell behind only *Ladies' Home Journal* and *Comfort* and it was fourth in line in 1895 with 600,000 subscribers (Mott, vol. III, 6; vol. IV, 16–17).

The *Companion* achieved its phenomenal success by marketing itself to a dual audience of parents and juvenile readers. Capitalizing on the "companion" metaphor as a "helper" to parents and "friend" to youth, the *Companion* purported both implicitly and explicitly to edify juveniles with wholesome ideas that were packaged in a way they would nonetheless enjoy. Such a marketing ploy was invested with liberal doses of idealism. It appealed to parents' sentimentalized sense of themselves as good and proper guardians of youth; it appealed to romantic notions of the home as the hallowed space where values and correct ideas were imparted; and it approached juveniles as precocious and adventurous beings who would nevertheless turn out right under the guidance of their reputable Victorian families.

Northern periodical editors of the genteel tradition, of which the *Companion* was a part, imagined those families — their readership — as white, middle-class, Anglo-Saxon Protestants, and the morals to the stories therein defaulted to that assumption. Thus, the racial implications of Chopin's marketing her work through even a covertly didactic venue such as the *Companion* suggests that her stories had the potential to be read as more than simply lessons on Louisianians' racial identities. As morals to (imagined, if not in fact) *white* readers, they circulated as behavior manuals for a social order that was hierarchized with the "whitest" people at the top and the "blackest" at the bottom. Upper orders were responsible for those below; lower orders were to respect their superiors.

Even if "lower orders" were not reading the *Companion*, such stories set up expectations for proper nonwhite subordination and drew conceptions about non-Wasps, especially if readers had little contact with people unlike themselves against which to measure the veracity of such representations. Hence, one of the primary legacies of Chopin's *Companion* stories is the record they leave us of how people were taught to treat one another as a result of their distance from what the *Companion* normalized as a standard Wasp American identity.

This provocative idea — that Chopin's *Companion* stories endure as artifacts of those values an adult community wished to pass on it its youth — deserves attention. Chapter 1 revisits late nineteenth-century constructions of female authorship to rethink canonical explanations of the motives and intent fueling Chopin's literary production. Northern periodical editors' attraction to regionalism's aesthetics, which called for faithful renderings of life by writers deemed credible to speak about that region's peoples, determined in large part Chopin's choice of "local color" subject matter.[5] Furthermore, opportunities for women's writing for juvenile periodicals in general, and the high circulation of the *Companion* in particular, matched Chopin's ambition for her stories to be commercially successful and hence influenced her drawing of plots and characters.

Chapter 2 addresses Chopin's engagement with the history of the Creoles in particular, but also the Cajuns, in the latter decades of the nineteenth century. Through close textual readings of Chopin's first three *Companion* texts, "For Marse Chouchoute," "A Wizard from Gettysburg," and "A Rude Awakening," chapter 2 demonstrates how Chopin, in these early stories, self-consciously produces the Creole and the Cajun as distinct ethnic categories of white identity distinguished by their respective bourgeois and hireling/laboring-class socioeconomic stratification.

Chapter 3 illustrates how Chopin employed conventions from the traditions of children's literature and sentimental fiction to tailor her local color politics in five *Companion* tales — "A Matter of Prejudice," "Loka," "Beyond the Bayou," "Mamouche," and "Polydore" — specifically for the genteel juvenile periodical market.

And chapter 4 addresses the many stories Chopin authored or submitted for publication after *The Awakening*, among them "Aunt Lympy's

Interference," "The Wood-Choppers," "Polly," and most important, "Charlie." The most extensive treatment to date of this post-*Awakening* novella interprets "Charlie" as Chopin's self-conscious fictional antidote to *The Awakening*'s faults, a compromise tale that mitigates authorial rebuke by embodying gender transgression in the young Creole woman Charlotte Laborde instead of the more American, Kentucky Protestant Edna Pontellier.

Coloring
Locals

1

Kate Chopin's Canonical and Market Place
Authorship, Authorization, and Authority

Since the Norwegian scholar Per Seyersted made *The Complete Works of Kate Chopin* available in 1969, academics have been trying to figure out what Chopin — like her character Edna — "was up to" when she wrote her two novels and many short stories about life in rural, post-Reconstruction Louisiana.[1] From statements on book banning and literary expulsion to accounts of a post-*Awakening* depression that curtailed any further literary production, early narratives have circulated about Chopin's life and work that later scholars have seen fit to revise.[2]

Some of this confusion about Chopin's life and work is a direct result of her own unreliable self-representation as a woman writer at the fin de siècle. Chopin's *Book News* rejoinder to condemnatory reviews of *The Awakening*, where she disavows responsibility for the deliberate choices she made in writing Edna's story, and her *St. Louis Post-Dispatch* essay "On Certain Brisk, Bright Days," where she deadpans that her writing is a mere substitute for the seductions of housework, are just two examples of the searing wit, sarcasm, and sardonic humor that we now recognize as characteristic of Chopin's public, nonliterary writing, writing that many early scholars and contemporaneous reviewers trusted at face value.

One way of unpacking Chopin's complex narrative voice is to contextualize her as a female author whose sense of self was deeply invested in the South.[3] As a writer negotiating the stringent constraints of *southern womanhood* — "an extreme version of the nineteenth-century lady" — Chopin was forced to develop tropes of female authorship that allowed her to straddle the contradictions between dominant definitions of "woman" and "writer" in late nineteenth-century America (Jones 5). Because such feminine ideals as privacy, domesticity, reproductivity, docility, dependence, and self-effacement conflicted necessarily with the public, commercial, productive, active, independent, and self-promotive demands of writing and publishing fiction, female authors throughout the nineteenth century were commonly engaged in narrative subterfuges of authorial self-representation to assure their readership that their writing did not compromise their womanhood.[4]

These female authors of fiction, then, fabricated a split identity to accommodate the nineteenth-century oxymoron "woman writer." Scholars have commonly figured this separation between an artificial public and authentic private self as a process of "masking," whereby women "wore" an acceptable face in order to hide their unacceptable career ambitions. The language of masking is also used to describe fictions said to excuse particularly white female characters' gender transgressions by subsuming such errant behaviors in marriage plots or other traditional, albeit punishing, formulae (Jones 39).

Masking as a metaphor for surface conformity has additionally been articulated by scholars of early and late nineteenth-century women's literature as a practice of subversion, whereby even stories that end in conventional marriage plots may be said to be "subversive" at those moments when female heroines undercut or upset orthodox patriarchal norms. Subversion as a critical term and reading strategy has been important in the revaluation and canonization of women's fiction and has been deployed as an indispensable model for reading and writing about texts authored by women.[5]

Consequently, Kate Chopin, too, has been valued for the subversive qualities of her fiction. Some members of the respected "first wave" of Chopin scholars writing in the 1970s and 1980s such as Emily Toth, Barbara Ewell, and Peggy Skaggs, as well as later ones such as Ellen Peel, have articulated subversion as a useful and important way to talk about Chopin's texts, with their often conflicting messages written into ambiguous, unfinished, or surprise endings.

However, the critical discourse of subversion has occasionally given way to an erroneous myth of transcendence claiming that Chopin's liberal sexual politics transcend their time and place rather than develop squarely within the Woman Question debate, the polarities of which can be accounted for by the discursive constructs of the traditional True Woman on the one hand and the reformist New Woman on the other.[6]

Furthermore, this narrative of transcendence has been extended to Chopin's racial politics, so that Chopin's progressive position on gender has been applied to her representations of race and ethnicity as well.[7] Chopin's local color tales are often spoken of as being sympathetic to the plight of Louisiana people of color, especially female African Americans, Creoles, and Cajuns, and she is celebrated for her willingness to expose the injustices these people suffer and to champion their triumphs.

Except that in Chopin's fiction, Creoles and Cajuns are white. I am therefore suspicious of readings that do not take into account the ways in which Chopin's gender and class representations work together distinctly to construct race and/or produce ethnic identity.[8] To read Chopin's articulations of identity categories as operating independently of one another leaves us asking, "Was Chopin a feminist or was she not?" when we try to reconcile such contradictions as Lolotte's conventional femininity in "A Rude Awakening" with Edna's unorthodox female self in *The Awakening*, as well as "Was Chopin a racist or was she not?" when we discover sympathetic and racist impulses operating simultaneously in "Loka" and "Beyond the Bayou."

Questioning Chopin's racial liberalism is itself a bold act, for it threatens to jeopardize the hard-won successes of an entire generation of Chopin scholars, researchers to whom all successive Chopin students are indebted because they have been handed Chopin and her canonical status on a silver platter. In an essay that came after nearly two decades of Chopin scholarship, just as a second wave of scholars began questioning earlier assumptions, Emily Toth, one of today's foremost Chopin scholars and biographers, publicly voiced a frustration with newer scholars who challenged Chopin's reputation as a racial sympathizer. In an essay that came at a pivotal moment in the history of Chopin scholarship, Toth defends Chopin's racial politics and, notably, does so through the metaphor of masking:

Kate Chopin herself translated her social criticism. Because her local color characters were quaint, distant, and sometimes women of color as well, they were less threatening to mainstream audiences if they did unconventional things — such as indulging in sex outside marriage or criticizing patriarchal norms. *This kind of masking* [emphasis added], sometimes attributed to local color writers of the late nineteenth century, is actually much, much older: even Shakespeare and his contemporaries set thinly disguised portrayals of current chicanery in ancient Rome or Italy or Spain. Besides being prudent, these disguises gave certain audiences a pleasing sense that they were in the know — and Chopin's readers, at least today, recognize the powerful feminist messages delivered in such seemingly quaint stories as "Désirée's Baby" and "La Belle Zoraïde." ("Introduction," *Louisiana Literature* [Spring 1994] 14)

Invaluable as Toth's research continues to be for modern-day Chopin students, this essay marks a relative dividing point between first- and second-wave approaches to reading, teaching, writing about, and valuing Chopin.[9] Swelling this second wave was Helen Taylor in 1989, followed by Michele Birnbaum in 1994 and Sandra Gunning in 1995. Their position — that although Chopin may have been nonconformist on issues of gender, she was thoroughly orthodox on issues of race — constitute precisely those ideas Toth responds to in her comments.

However, Toth's defense claims for Chopin and her readers concurrent, irreconcilable racist and antiracist impulses. On the one hand, to say that Chopin deliberately couched threatening (white) feminist behavior in nonthreatening, colored female bodies is to say that women of color were viewed as being essentially different from white women; otherwise, representing gender transgression in colored female bodies would be just as scandalous as doing the same in white counterparts. On the other hand, to suggest that white female readers could ascertain such (colored) representations as mere surfaces of difference overlaying cores of (white) sameness is to argue that white female readers identified with essential likenesses of themselves beneath colored fronts or veneers.

Ultimately, Toth settles the debate on Chopin's racial politics not on the letter of Chopin's texts themselves but on the very issue of whether one should even speak of racism in tandem with Chopin. "Literary criticism," Toth writes, "is not particularly effective in creating social change" ("Introduction" 17), a pronouncement that works to foreclose any further discussion of Chopin's constructions of race and, presumably, gender, class, and ethnicity as well. For by distinguishing the literary from the social, Toth is able to shift her focus from understanding the fiction writer to censoring the critic. Her rhetoric, which exhibits a desire to rescue Chopin from the charge of racism, further hints at a fear that the taint of racism may devalue Chopin's position within the American literary canon.

Of second-wave scholars, it is Gunning who most directly addresses the reluctance on the part of practitioners of white academic feminism to acknowledge Chopin's racial articulations and who allays fears of Chopin's devaluation by pointing out the value in historically sensitive assessments of her work, claiming "there is nothing to fear in fully examining both the potentials — and the complications — that inhere uneasily in the female radicalism of literary subjects such as Kate Chopin. . . . [Her] value is precisely the troublesomeness of her antipatriarchal stance that emerges, paradoxically, through her embrace of white privilege" (*Race* 142–43).

Hence are the two traditions to which all subsequent Chopin scholarship is beholden. Now fully vested in the history of American letters, we may turn our attention to Chopin's fiction that does not precisely fit the metanarratives of either first- or second-wave scholarship about her life and work. By studying those eleven short stories Chopin originally published in the *Youth's Companion*, I hope to examine not only how Chopin's fictions instructed their primarily non-southern readership to apprehend Louisiana peoples' richly complex identities through racialized, classed, and gendered markers but also how her advancement of white supremacy, specifically through Creoles and Cajuns, required her to rely upon the period's conservative articulations of masculinity and femininity.

I begin by addressing Chopin's reasons for turning to periodical writing in the first place.

FEMALE AUTHORSHIP AND AUTHORIZATION

Although Chopin's recognition within American literary studies derives in large part from the importance of her third and final novel, *The Awakening*,[10] Chopin was primarily known to and valued by her reading audience as an author of short fiction, and she was remembered in critical histories for some thirty years after her death for her accomplishments in the genre.[11]

Chopin was a short story writer by both necessity and choice. She wrote in a day when, as her predecessor Margaret Fuller observed, periodicals were the "only efficient instrument," not only through which readers could receive material but also through which authors could disseminate it. As a medium, the periodical was particularly hospitable to women, in part because the short story form that the periodical featured was becoming feminized as a literary genre. Attitudes that Susan Koppelman expresses about the short story today — that it suffers from "a loss of status, currently being viewed by many in the literary world as an apprenticeship genre, preparation for fiction writers on their way to tackling the greater task of writing novels" (799) — were under construction at the very moment when Chopin was writing. Chopin's contemporary, William Dean Howells, one of the period's most influential magazine editors and proponents of realism, was in fact actively feminizing short story writing as he worked concomitantly to masculinize novel writing (Kaplan 15–43). His construction of the short story as a gendered genre coincided with "the growth of the magazine industry['s] . . . inexhaustible market for stories oriented toward specific audiences" (Koppelman 802), so that opportunities for women's writing increased as venues for gendered writing — ladies' fashion magazines, family papers, and juvenile periodicals — emerged. Such market conditions have led Koppelman to conclude that "the fact that so many [women writers] settled on the short story as the literary form in which to develop their greatest skills had as much to do with the popularity of the genre and their consequent greater financial opportunities as it did with creative inclination" (799).

In addition to general marketplace opportunities, periodical writing conveniently provided female authors with a façade behind which to camouflage any concerns that their writing might compromise their womanhood. Because writing periodical fiction allowed women to perform their work within the confines of their domestic locus, it appeared that such work did not conflict with a woman's primary duties as wife and mother. Because such traditional roles were assumed to be a woman's first priority, periodical writing could be promoted as a hobby along the lines of cross-stitch, an amusement that was effortlessly performed during leisured hours amidst much activity and interruption by family members.[12]

One standard strategy women used to break into periodical writing was to begin with juvenile periodicals, the least-threatening and least-questioned venue of publishing for women because childcare was Victorian woman's quintessential concern. Particularly new and unknown women writers initially published in highly acclaimed and widely circulating children's periodicals to catch the attention of prominent adult magazine editors and eventually break into other fiction markets.[13] These women "capitalized upon woman's traditional relation to children and the home. They were, in fact, ingenious entrepreneurs" (Benardete and Moe 9).

Whether Chopin was doing so consciously or simply following an established career path for women, she relied on juvenile periodicals to serve as her stepping-stone to broader literary acclaim. Chopin gained her national reputation first and foremost as a writer for juvenile periodicals. Between 1891 and 1902 Chopin successfully placed one story in *Wide Awake*, four in *Harper's Young People*, and eleven, including her last, in the *Youth's Companion*.[14] She earned $787 from these magazines ($750 from the *Youth's Companion* alone), a sum that makes up over one-third of her lifetime's $2300 literary income.[15]

But both the ideological and market conditions of Chopin's day required business savvy for success, especially if a woman writer did not have a personal relationship with a male editor to escort her into the field, which Chopin did not. In her article "Kate Chopin and Editors, 'A Singular Class of Men,'" Phyllis Vanlandingham denies Chopin such savvy when she addresses the 1897 essay Chopin published in the *St. Louis Criterion*, in which Chopin expresses her frustration with male editors. Chopin wrote:

[E]ditors are really a singular class of men; they have such strange and incomprehensible ways with them.

I once submitted a story to a prominent New York editor, who returned it promptly with the observation that "the public is getting very tired of that sort of thing." I felt very sorry for the public, but I wasn't willing to take one man's word for it, so I clapped the offensive document into an envelope and sent it away again — this time to a well-known Boston editor.

"I am delighted with the story," read the letter of acceptance, which came a few weeks later, "and so, I am sure, will be our readers."

When an editor says a thing like that it is at his own peril. I at once sent him another tale, thinking thereby to increase his delight and add to it ten-fold.

"Can you call this a story, dear madam?" he asked when he sent it back. "Really, there seems to me to be no story at all; what is it all about?" I could see his pale smile.

It was getting interesting, like playing at battledore and shuttlecock. Off went the would-be story by the next mail to the New York editor — the one who so considerately gauged the ennui of the public.

"It is a clever and excellent piece of work," he wrote me; "the story is well told." I wonder if the editor, the writer and the public are ever at one.[16]

Although not often discussed critically, Vanlandingham's essay stands, figuratively, at the height of narratives implying Chopin's "fortunate naïveté" as an uncalculating writer, an image Chopin herself set forth in her authorial self-representations when she claimed she was entirely at the mercy of "unconscious selection" for her fiction, and other such myths (*CW* 722). Similarly, Vanlandingham's article celebrates an assumption that Chopin and her editors were seldom "at one," claiming that such symbiosis would have foreclosed the possibility of Chopin's ever writing daring texts such as "The Storm" or *The Awakening*. Vanlandingham thus concludes that readers should "be thankful that [Chopin], unlike Grace King and many of her contemporaries, continued to find editors 'strange and incomprehensible'" (166).

Such an argument necessarily centers around the following broad — and dubious — assumptions: that periodical publishing practices did not influence Chopin's literary production and that in fact she was completely oblivious to, uninformed about, or unconcerned with a periodical's target audience. Vanlandingham's article reaches conclusions such as: "[W]ith few exceptions, [Chopin] wrote to please herself and then tried to find publishers for her work" (159); "some of Chopin's problems with editors stemmed from her failure to consider the audience a magazine or journal was designed to reach" (162); and "she simply sent her work wherever she wanted to see it published, without worrying about the periodical's audience, editorial policies, or esthetic principles" (163).

However, Chopin's Account/Memo books — in which she meticulously logged by hand the submission, rejection, and acceptance dates of most of her stories, along with their remuneration — indicate the contrary. For instance, to make her point, Vanlandingham uses the example of the story "Lilacs," which Chopin finally sold to the *New Orleans Times-Democrat* after unsuccessful attempts to place it elsewhere. Admittedly, Chopin's business sense in marketing "Lilacs" is difficult to defend. Vanlandingham accurately cites Chopin's illogic in sending her manuscript both to the "highly ethical *Century* . . . and to the decadent, antiestablishment *Yellow Book*" (162), a premiere genteel periodical on the one hand and an avant-garde art press on the other.

But Vanlandingham's reconstructed history tells only part of the story. Chopin's logbooks document that the *Century* was the first and the *Yellow Book* the last of eight consecutive submissions Chopin made, sending out her manuscript to groups of ideologically compatible publications. Choosing the most prestigious — and most conventional — genteel periodicals first and then moving on to nonliterary ladies' magazines where she had had some success before finally approaching the (long-shot) innovative art presses, Chopin in fact sent her manuscript to the *Century*, *Atlantic*, *Scribner's*, and *Harper's* and then to *Vogue*, *Cosmopolitan*, and finally the *Chap-Book* and *Yellow Book* before placing it with the *New Orleans Times-Democrat*.[17]

Thus, Chopin's logbooks demonstrate that there was some form of logical consistency to her marketing strategy, regardless of how misguided that plan of action was. For "Lilacs," as it turns out, was hardly suitable for any periodical of the Gilded Age, not because Chopin wrote a story about illicit sexual activity and female sexual longing, as she did in published stories such as "La Belle Zoraïde" and "At the 'Cadian Ball," but because she represented such longing as same-sex desire between women.

With the exception of Thomas Bonner, scholars have not addressed the explicitly homosocial environment of the convent or the homoerotic attachment between the former convent school-girl-turned-actress Adrienne Farival and one of the Sacred Heart nuns, Sister Agathe.[18] Although the homosocial world of female "love and ritual" was still accepted and practiced in the late-Victorian era when Chopin was writing, the homosexual attraction between Adrienne and Agathe in "Lilacs" clearly deviated from this norm and would have been read as an aberration of female friendship that had crossed the line, so to speak, into the realm of the perverted.[19]

Furthermore, Vanlandingham reads in Chopin's note that accompanied the manuscript of "Lilacs" to the *Chap-Book* a "naïveté" that goes hand in hand with her alleged disregard for a periodical's audience. Vanlandingham notes that when Chopin sent "Lilacs" along with "Three Portraits" and two poems to the *Chap-Book*, she expressed in the most indiscreet terms her eagerness to be published therein. Chopin wrote, "I would greatly like to see one of [my writings] — some of them — something — anything over my name in the *Chap-Book*" (162). Although one cannot dispute Chopin's desire evident in the letter, her so-called naïveté can more accurately be described as the weary experience of rejection, especially when the *Chap-Book* letter is juxtaposed with the sentiments expressed in her essay "A Singular Class of Men." Looking back, then, to that same essay, we can read in her sarcasm not a genuine bewilderment of acceptable standards for fiction writing but a frustration with the politics that regulated her authorial success: the arbitrariness of individual judgement and the fact that her access to publication was so thoroughly controlled by editors who for the most part were male.

Given her cultural milieu, then, it is not surprising that Chopin found the most accepting forum for her bold themes of female autonomy and sexual desire in a magazine edited by another woman. Josephine Redding, the editor-in-chief of the ladies' fashion magazine *Vogue*, printed nineteen of Chopin's manuscripts, the largest number of short stories published by any single periodical in Chopin's lifetime. *Vogue* and Chopin were indeed "at one" in their nineteenth-century feminist politics for white, middle-to-upper-middle-class women. In 1894 the magazine made this editorial statement regarding fictional portrayals of female love and romance: "The pink and white — débutante afternoon tea — atmosphere in which convention says we must present love, means intellectual asphyxiation for us."[20] Clearly *Vogue*, like Chopin, was interested in representing women as sexual beings.

By the time *Vogue* made such a public statement, Chopin had already learned that it was the showcase in which she could count on placing her "experimental" feminist fiction. Between 1892 and 1895 *Vogue* was either Chopin's first- or second-choice periodical for publishing much of her fiction, indicating the author was both tracking and targeting the markets in which she would be most successful. In those three years Chopin sent first to *Vogue*, whose editor accepted the following manuscripts upon first submission: "Désirée's Baby," "Caline," "Two Summers and Two Souls," "Ripe Figs," "A Lady of Bayou St. John," "La Belle Zoraïde," "A Respectable Woman," and "The Kiss"; and upon having a first-choice periodical reject a manuscript, she sent out to *Vogue* as her second-choice publisher these manuscripts: "A Visit to Avoyelles," "The Unexpected," "The Letters," and "Dr. Chevalier's Lie," all of which the periodical also published.[21]

But there were reasons why Chopin was sending only her most experimental fiction to *Vogue*, why she didn't want to stake her literary reputation on her success with this one magazine, and why, once established as a writer, she later attempted to broaden her market by sending her work to other, more distinguished presses before resorting to *Vogue* as her ace in the hole. Unlike the period's genteel periodicals, which prided themselves on the notoriety of their fiction, *Vogue* was a society and fashion magazine (Mott, vol. IV, 756–62). Its readership was the tony New York set (and those who wished to read about it), so the magazine did not serve as a stepping-stone toward broader literary acclaim; as an added disincentive, *Vogue* paid relatively little for fiction.[22]

Thus, in addition to her relationship with *Vogue*, Chopin cultivated an amicable relationship with a second periodical. That was the *Youth's Companion*.[23] Between 1891 and 1902 the *Companion* bought twenty of Chopin's short stories, published eleven of them, and paid her anywhere from $15 to $65 for each manuscript, a tidy sum compared to *Vogue*'s pay range of between $3 and $25 per story.[24] "For Marse Chouchoute," Chopin's first *Companion* piece, appeared only twenty months after she debuted "Wiser Than a God" in the *Philadelphia Musical Journal*. And after *The Awakening* was published in 1899, the *Companion* was one of two periodicals to remain a loyal vehicle for Chopin's work. While *Vogue* published its last Chopin tale, "The White Eagle," on 12 July 1900, the *Companion* accepted Chopin's last two stories to appear in print during her lifetime: "The Wood-Choppers," 29 May, and "Polly," 3 July, both in 1902.[25]

In the latter decades of the nineteenth century, when Chopin was writing and marketing her work, the *Companion* was a veritable bastion of the publishing industry. Not only the longest-running periodical in America, the *Companion* was also among the most widely circulating.[26] Begun by Nathaniel Willis and Asa Rand in 1827 as a Sunday School weekly reader, the four-page weekly folio was a children's "companion" to one of the most important religious newspapers of the age, the Boston *Recorder*. Not surprisingly, the material in the early *Companion* reflected its somber Puritan roots and the heavily didactic tradition of eighteenth-century children's literature.

In 1857 Willis and Rand sold the *Companion* to the partnership of John W. Olmstead and Daniel Sharp Ford, the latter of whom took sole ownership of the *Companion* in 1867. Ford increased the *Companion*'s then 48,000 circulation figure to more than 500,000 by the mid-1890s, accomplishing this monumental feat through many methods.

Low subscription rates certainly accounted in part for the *Companion*'s popularity, especially in America's heartland. Between 1891 and 1902 the *Companion* sold for five cents an issue or $1.75 annually — half the price of the period's genteel adult literary magazines. The only records now available show that the *Companion* circulated via subscription in rural midwestern and Pacific northwestern states such as Colorado, Illinois, Indiana, Michigan, Ohio, and Oregon, as well as such urban eastern states as Connecticut, Maryland, Massachusetts, New Jersey, New York, and Rhode Island (Cutts, introduction, xii).

Ford was able to keep subscription prices low by being among the period's first editors to sell ads to offset his magazine's printing costs. He further instituted a "premiums system," whereby current subscribers received prizes for selling additional subscriptions. But two other changes Ford made in the *Companion*'s content were just as important, if not critical, avenues to the magazine's phenomenal success. First, he began to

value a model of children's literature that more closely imitated adult fiction. By means of this move, Ford facilitated his second tactic: He broadened the magazine's audience base to include the composite age groups and sexes of the entire Victorian American family.

Regardless of actual readership demographics, which are scanty at best, Ford's *imagined* concept of his audience most profoundly influenced his editorial policy. Ford thought of his readership primarily as inhabitants of the *home*, a space he, in keeping with conservative contemporaneous discourses, idealized as a nourishing and purifying sphere presided over by the angelic Victorian mother. Like the period's very definition of idealized womanhood, Ford's sentimentalized home space and the inhabitants within bespoke their assumed whiteness as fully enfranchised American citizens; consequently, both their adherence to conservative middle-class gender norms and his editorial policy defaulted to those assumptions. Idealizing readers as members of a pure and innocent (white, American) family suggested the reciprocal value of subscribing to the magazine. While the product itself worked to inculcate norms regarding what good families and their members should strive to be, receiving the periodical said something flattering about household members as *Youth's Companion* readers.

As with nonfiction articles, fiction was accepted and rejected on the basis of its "appropriateness" for the respectable American Victorian household and its influence on impressionable young readers. R. Gordon Kelly's valuable work on the *Companion's* history documents that Ford influenced the production of material that potential contributors wrote for the *Companion* by sending them a leaflet detailing what it would and would not publish. Quoting from such a leaflet mailed out in the 1890s, Kelly writes:

[Ford] insisted on stories that "stirred an admiration for healthy thinking and brave action" and contained authoritative facts. He emphasized movement and dramatic effectiveness and called for stories that had "well-devised [plots] and at least one strong incident" but were untainted by sensationalism, melodrama, or improper language. Detective stories, a staple of the dime-novel industry, were proscribed, as were love stories. Crime was acceptable if it was necessary to a story, but it was to be kept in the background, and all unpleasant or unwholesome details were to be omitted; neither bloodshed nor "evil Passions" were permitted prominence. "The moral tone of the stories must be irreproachable," Ford admonished in a leaflet sent to possible contributors. Final impressions of death or unrelieved calamity conflicted with the *Companion*'s desire to convey cheer; pathetic stories were required to turn toward "brightened endings." . . . An ethical purpose was always desirable, but the moral was to be revealed "by the story itself, not by any comment of the writer." (*Mother* 12–13)

In addition to the leaflet, there is further evidence that suggests just how consciously Ford and his staff of largely anonymous editors influenced a priori the production of literature for their particular publication. A collection of unpublished letters written by William Henry Rideing, an editor at the *Companion* in Boston, to William Morris Colles, a literary agent in London who brokered British stories to the *Companion* as well as fiction already published in the *Companion* to British periodicals, reveals how editorial policy shaped the final versions of pieces merely proposed to the magazine and how the gatekeeping process of acceptance and rejection determined what type of material potential contributors would come to associate with its title. From his office in Boston, Rideing wrote a letter dated 6 December 1894, stating: "if he cares to submit a few sketches of his adventures to the *Companion* we will consider them and pay at the rate of £10 per 1000 for them, provided they are acceptable. Each sketch should not be more than 2,000 or 2,500 words in length."

In another letter dated 26 December 1894, Rideing wrote:

Dear Mr. Colles:-

I fear I cannot make an offer for the story of Miss Harraden, unless we can see it beforehand. The *Companion*'s short stories never succeed 3,500 words in length, and its serials usually run to 15,000 [sic] in five chapters of 3,000 words each. If you think it would suit a young audience whose parents object to the portrayal of passion, and who must have children (not babies) portrayed as children, please let us see the MS. A love story would never do for us, however.

Then in a letter dated 21 January 1895, Rideing advised:

> Dear Mr. Colles:-
>
> We might use some fragments of your "first white man" incidents of adventure and illustrations of customs, not too grewsome [sic] for young people — but he would have to wait at least a year before we could print anything.

And finally, in a letter dated 31 July 1895, he briefly stated:

> Dear Mr. Colles:-
>
> Sir Lewis Morris's verses are excellent, but not quite suited to a juvenile publication like the *Companion*.
>
> Thank you for offering them. I am
>
> Yours faithfully
William H. Rideing[27]

The Rideing letters demonstrate Ford's guiding editorial policy: that he saw the *Companion* as a morally upright publication whose aim was partly to interest juveniles and partly to acquire the approval of those same juveniles' parents. The *Youth's Companion*'s marked success can be attributed in large part to this broad, multiaudience appeal.[28] It attempted to provide, in good Arnoldian fashion, a family-friendly version of "the best that [was] known and thought in the world" for all family readers.[29] Renowned authors and poets such as Harriet Beecher Stowe, Elizabeth Stuart Phelps, Mary E. Wilkins Freeman, Sarah Orne Jewett, Alfred Lord Tennyson, Henry Wadsworth Longfellow, and Walt Whitman each contributed to the *Companion*.[30] Similarly, articles on timely topics such as science, health, the environment, education, politics, and current events, though written at a young-adult reading level, were nonetheless authored by leaders in these fields, among them Theodore Roosevelt, Grover Cleveland, Booker T. Washington, Henry M. Stanley, Lillian Nordica, and P. T. Barnum.[31] And advertisements for medicinal remedies, household and garden instruments, and adult male and female hygiene products clearly were directed at parents rather than their children.

Thus, regardless of its front-page profile as a *youth's* companion, the periodical was in fact marketed to a mixed audience of children, young adults, and adults, a deliberate targeting strategy that gave it as much in common with the adult, "genteel" periodicals of the Gilded Age, such as the *Century*, *Scribner's*, *Harper's*, and the *Atlantic*, as with magazines more exclusively targeted at young readers, such as *Our Young Folk* and *St. Nicholas*. Indeed, Carol Klimick Cyganowski's study of the genteel periodical tradition in America emphasizes that such genres were not so far apart. Cyganowski points to the overlap between these magazines' self-image and that of more "bonafide" family papers, such as the *Saturday Evening Post*. She describes genteel periodicals as "a literary product for home consumption [with a self-conscious understanding] that the audience within that home is comprised of children and adolescents as well as adults. . . . [T]he magazines early engaged themselves as providers of a composite product which supplied good value in assuring quality reading for every member of the family" (314).

Cyganowski's insertion of the modifier "quality" to describe "reading for every member of the family" points to the dual mission such periodicals set out to fulfill: They intended to provide "highbrow" reading that met the age groups and interests of all members of the family, as well as morally upright texts that were appropriate for a family's composite ages and sexes. These publications were subliminal etiquette guides in their portrayals of proper courtship behavior; deference to one's betters in age, class, and race; and, of course, correct gender performance for both young men and women.

Even though much has been written about the period's concern for the influence of reading on young women, Cyganowski's assertion that editors were as much concerned with the effect their printed material had on the young male reader is supported by an incident involving the *Century* in the mid-1880s. After the magazine started the serial printing of a novel whose plot involved the hero's romantic attachment to a married woman, "subscribers and the press waged a war of complaint against the novel, the novelist, the magazine, and the magazine editor which can justifiably be seen as emblematic of the risk American magazines ran in affronting middle American sexual morality in the nineteenth century. [The editor, Richard Watson Gilder] felt the criticism was justified, given the image and role of the family magazine, and asked [the author] for changes" (199). Thus, the (adult) genteel periodicals and (juvenile) family magazines were in some ways flip sides of the same coin: Family magazines directed largely at juveniles were concerned with interesting adult readers, whereas adult periodicals were ever conscious of the fact that their material was available to younger members of the household.

The *Companion*'s self-identification began to reflect its multi-age marketing strategy more prominently as the years progressed. Although throughout its history the magazine maintained a front-page profile as a *youth's* companion, the words "a family paper" began appearing regularly on a back-page editorial statement in 1865, as a subtitle on page six of each issue in the mid-1890s, and as part of the masthead in 1903. Thus, editor Ford continued to increase the *Companion*'s circulation not only by attracting new generations of subscribers but also by retaining previous ones who, though having outgrown an exclusively juvenile product, nonetheless appreciated a paper "for all the family."

By constructing texts suitable for more than one market, Chopin was able to submit her manuscripts to other "adult" periodicals in addition to the *Companion*. By dramatizing her concerns within familial settings and variously aged bodies, Chopin blanketed the publication markets of both adult and juvenile magazines and thus created better odds for placing her fiction. Although as a lesser-known female writer she was more easily authorized to write for — and had reasons for desiring that her work be published in — the *Youth's Companion*, Chopin's fiction was eminently suitable for a variety of genteel, family, and juvenile publications alike. I turn now to why these publications exhibited "a marked degree of editorial continuity" (Kelly 3).

FEMALE AUTHORITY

In her highly regarded study of the nineteenth-century literary marketplace, Susan Coultrap-McQuin locates the roots of the "genteel" image so common to the period's quality magazines in the prominence of a central ideal: that of the Gentleman Publisher. According to Coultrap-McQuin, it was the operating code of the Gentleman Publisher that made editors "adopt the paternalistic role of moral guardian" toward female and juvenile readers, who were assumed to be in need of protection (46). Although the Gentleman Publisher, an obviously white, upper-middle-class construct of heterosexual masculinity, held its greatest currency in the middle part of the century, most of the men who embraced and promoted the ideal began working in the book trade much earlier in the antebellum period. These early nineteenth-century publishers were like their eighteenth-century counterparts in that, even though they were skilled tradesmen in the printing and selling of books, they lacked any familial connection to fortune or title and therefore belonged, by and large, to the skilled trades class. Thus, the designation of "Gentleman Publisher" appealed to early-nineteenth-century publishers for the connections it made between their trade and the genteel world of culture, education, and refinement.

But the ideal's specific rise in the nineteenth century came about because of market conditions that had not existed a century earlier. "Between 1820 and 1850 the publishing industry expanded tenfold in response to increasing national levels of literacy, people's growing interest in reading as cheap entertainment, and an expanding railroad system making national distribution of books possible" (Coultrap-McQuin 30). Because competition for manuscripts was fierce and piracy rampant, publishers instituted the principle of trade courtesy as a means toward voluntarily regulating the industry in an era before substantial copyright law. "Trade courtesy was the practice of respecting the prior rights of another firm to an author's works . . . [so that] when an intention to publish was announced, other firms would agree not to publish a rival edition or to bargain for that writer's future work" (Coultrap-McQuin 30). One publisher was noted as saying of his colleagues: "No one of them [Putnam, Appleton, Harper, Scribner] or of a few more, would go for another's author any more than for his watch" (qtd. in Kelly, *Mother* 10).

This gentleman's agreement of trade courtesy, which Coultrap-McQuin isolates as the beginning of the Gentleman Publisher ideal, served many purposes. It transformed the tradesman-bookseller of the eighteenth century into the polished gentleman of the nineteenth, who, though lacking fortune and distinguished family background, could nonetheless lay claim to gentility through his civilized business practices and polite personal behaviors. Once trade courtesy had become an established practice, the ideal of the Gentleman Publisher remained attractive to periodical editors in the latter decades of the century because, as successful men of the business world whose new fortunes were significantly less than those of rising industrial magnates, their genteel behavior explained their lower income through the claim that their profits suffered from the absence of crude and ruthless business practices.

Although occasional unchecked marketplace competition may have influenced some dealings between periodical editors, by most accounts, polite agreements and voluntary restrictions characterized the great majority of business relations between them. R. Gordon Kelly quotes Donald Sheehan's assertion that the industry's leaders comprised the period's "most scrupulous men rather than its most grasping" (qtd. in Kelly, *Mother* 9). He further agrees with Sheehan's characterization of these men as "a reasonably homogeneous group which took pride in its conservatism. As pillars of the church and guardians of the family, they were as steadfastly traditional in their personal ideals as in their public convictions" (qtd. in Kelly, *Mother* 10).

The ideal of the Gentleman Publisher was an easy one for mid-nineteenth-century periodical editors to adopt because of its similarity to the already established ideal of the Christian Gentleman. As "pillars of the church and guardians of the family," white Anglo-Saxon Protestant Christianity was the background from which most of these men came. "Christian" and "gentleman" as modifiers of "publisher" heavily influenced these men's concepts of themselves and their material and editorial relationships with the public.

Daniel Sharp Ford was a paragon of this type of mid-nineteenth-century Christian gentleman publisher. Born on 5 April 1822 in Cambridge, Massachusetts, Ford grew up in a meager but devoutly Christian household that was fatherless from the time he was six months old. Through his own initiative, Ford acquired a common-school education and apprenticed himself as a printer. He secured work first as a compositor and then as a bookkeeper for the *Watchman and Reflector*, a weekly Baptist journal in Boston that he would later co-own with J. W. Olmstead.[32]

Ford's business and philanthropic efforts show that he maintained his commitment to the early conservatism of his youth throughout his life. When he acquired the *Youth's Companion* in 1857, the magazine still resembled its Congregationalist predecessor, the Boston *Recorder*. Although Ford transformed his new religious magazine into a secular publication, he nonetheless continued to dedicate the *Companion* to promoting these same principles through "gentry class values."[33]

As Kelly has already detailed, gentry class values were secularized manifestations of the same white, middle-to-upper-middle-class, Anglo-Saxon Protestantism that took specific shape in the genteel social types of the "gentleman" and the "lady." The principles of self-management required to emulate these social types, articulated by Kelly as "honesty, obedience, industry, and generosity" (*Mother* 6), were heralded as the guarantee against a fixed-class society. These gentry ideals promised that social status was no longer relegated to an accident of one's birth but rather could be achieved through methods of self-discipline and internal reform.

As themselves members of genteel society, Daniel Ford and his like-minded periodical editors had a vested interest in endorsing restraint and reform through gentlemanly conduct. Conflict between capital (the side to which these later editors belonged) and labor (the side of their employees) became rampant in the latter decades of the century, so much so that one periodical wrote of the times: "How to insure the worker the fruits of his labor is the social problem of today. . . . One can hardly listen to a speech or sermon, or direct his eyes to a page of current literature, without having this social question thrust upon him."[34] Labor strikes were common particularly in the North, where the nation's steel mills, coal mines, railroads, and various other industries were being built. As Gail Bederman has documented: "Beginning with the Great Uprising of 1877, the Gilded Age had seen an abundance of labor unrest. Between 1881 and 1905 there were nearly thirty-seven thousand strikes, often violent, involving seven million workers — an impressive number in a nation whose total work force in 1900 numbered only twenty-nine million" (14).

Three of the country's largest and bloodiest labor strikes took place between 1892 and 1894: the Homestead strike of steel mill workers, the Pullman strike of railway workers, and the great coal strike of 1894, this last of which involved two hundred thousand miners (Mott, vol. IV, 218–19). The debate surrounding these struggles was played out in the pages of America's mass media: the newspapers and periodicals. Genteel periodical editors paid attention to labor unrest as much from a sense of their own desire to maintain an existing social order as from their sense of responsibility to inform their reading public about issues of the day.

Consequently, the discursive antidote they prescribed for labor/capital strife was labor class obedience to capital class guidance through Christian submission. In his expressed concern for "the welfare of those who are dependent upon the returns from their daily toil for their livelihood," *Companion* editor Ford gave charitable donations of $50,000 a year during his lifetime, and $1 million at the time of his death, to the New England Baptist Church in support of its missionary efforts. According to one historical account, Ford believed "that the moment demanded closer personal relations between Christian business men and American workingmen, because of the workingman's 'religious indifference, his feverish unrest and his belief that business men and capital are his enemies. This attitude of mind,' [Ford] concluded, 'forbodes serious perils, and Christianity is the only influence that can change or modify them.'"[35]

Christianity, in this sense, euphemized passivity and peace in contrast to organized labor's active resistance. But the economic depression of the 1890s made many laborers impatient with the delayed promise of the American dream of social mobility through industry, self-discipline, and sacrifice. First- and second-generation Americans, whose immigrant forebears had paid for their children's improved social inheritance with their very lives, were particularly indignant because the American dream remained more elusive than obtainable to them.

In order to quell potential uprisings, genteel periodical editors endorsed contrasts between "American" and "un-American" behaviors, wherein energy-channeled-into-work connoted the former, and violence characterized the latter. Accurate as a perception or not, then, labor "agitators" became associated with, among other things, "foreignness," or all things *different* from a standard, middle-class, white Anglo-Saxon Protestant "American" code of conduct. As just one example of such difference and its connection with lower social status and the foreign-born, a *Life* cartoon satirized a labor protest. The drawing depicted labor leaders riding clouds around Heaven's gate while shouting in a nonstandard dialect, "We got da place picketed. Dey're usin' a non-union kind of harp in dere!"[36]

"The Labor Question" was just one manifestation of genteel periodical editors' larger concern with accommodating America's infinite differences in the Gilded Age. With sectional tensions still high between Union and Confederate sympathizers, immigration figures on the rise, and debates about the many "questions" ("The Labor Question," "The Woman Question," "The Negro Question") dividing the population along lines of class, race, and gender, genteel periodical editors responded to the many anxieties surrounding America's disunity by calling for "a sane and earnest Americanism" that sought "to increase the sentiment of union throughout our diverse sisterhood of States" (qtd. in Taylor 19).

Regional fiction answered this call for American unity by bringing to the fore a presence from the various regions of the country, and southern texts were particularly valued by northern editors.[37] Because the northern periodical press was eager to record the North's success of combining the formerly barbarous slaveholding Confederacy with the enlightened, racially tolerant Union, the "realist" aesthetics of regional fiction conveniently dovetailed with northern editors' desire for accurate pictures of southern life rendered through such "verifiable" means as scenic and dialectic depictions. Southerners were also quick to avail themselves of the opportunities afforded them by authoring their own stories; they were anxious to set "straight a record which, it was felt, had been left to the North to write" (Taylor 18).

Thus, by and large, southern authors' regionalist fictions were reconciliation texts that accomplished a dual agenda satisfactory to both sides: They assured the Union of its progress in establishing a peaceful, racially integrated New South, while they cleverly rewrote the Old South's social order into the New South's image. In southern reconciliation fiction, white men still played the role of the beneficent patriarchal southern master, whose right to political and social dominance was defended by African Americans' continued desire to serve him out of gratitude and innate dependency. Though such fictions were accepted by northern editors as mirror images of the often inaccessible backwater regions of the country, in the hands of southern writers, these stories became politically charged texts that often satisfied both northern desires for national harmony and southern needs to defend, if not preserve, the South's defeated past.

There are other reasons why northern periodical editors were all too happy to hand native southerners the authority to write the record on their region. One of those reasons was that the North had its own labor, racial, and gender problems to attend to at home. Another was the belief that the more remote the locale and the more removed its people and their customs, the less northern writers were capable of accessing and recording what they saw. Since at least the invention of the daguerreotype in 1839, practitioners of various forms of media and genres of writing in the United States and Europe, including photography, newsprint, the periodical press, literary criticism, poetry, and regional and realist fiction, argued their superiority via claims to mimesis.[38] Much like late-twentieth-century language used almost two hundred years later to separate "reliable" journalism from other types of writing, "truth," "fidelity," "objectivity," "accuracy," "perfect correspondence," "reflection," "mirror image," and even "disinterestedness" were just some of the terms used in the struggle for dominance of one media and/or genre of writing over another.[39]

Consequently, native southerners were invested with the authority to speak on the state of the South because, as mimetic "reporters," their intimate, first-hand knowledge of life around them lent them a credibility that outsiders lacked.[40] This construct of authorship — the fiction-writer-as-journalist — was particularly inviting to women because, to gain authority, women writers did not have to step outside the boundaries of their physical or metaphorical "place"; they simply were authorized to write about what they knew.[41] As "regional correspondents" for a northern-based media, these women writers' work — termed "local color" fiction by northern editors — gained authority through similar claims to mimetic representation.[42]

Helen Taylor's incisive commentary on local color writing demonstrates that northern periodical editors had yet another motive in mind when they accepted or solicited "realistic" regional texts from southern writers. Taylor argues that one of the main ideological functions of local color texts was to uphold the urban North as a hegemonic national center by marginalizing regions on the country's periphery:

> The words [local color] themselves, used by the northern literary establishment to define regional literature, speak their own ideological assumptions. *Local* denotes any "abnormal" literary subject decentered from the northeastern literary centers (especially Boston and New York) and far removed from northern industrial and commercial cities. The second word, *color*, indicates the exotic flavor required of such fiction. Not only must it provide a sense of lived experience in rural and small-town America; it must also construct those areas in ways that would confirm their very strangeness and curiosity to a "normal" northern reader. (17)

But as Amy Kaplan's important work on the discursive construction of the period's aesthetics demonstrates, that regional exoticism circulated only as a reflection of local people's exterior dissimilarity. Kaplan cogently argues that local color writing became a vogue subgenre within realist aesthetics because it created the fiction of a unified America: "[I]n a society of immigrants in which many Americans did not speak the same dialect, let alone the same language, a common language had to be constructed against the counterforces of foreign tongues and social fragmentation" (23). That "common [cross-cultural] language," she asserts, was the narrative of local color aesthetics, whose deployment of the "common," or average, not-noble man, who had "common," or universal, characteristics, was intended to promote a belief in the transhistorical and transcultural essence of human likeness existing beneath surfaces of difference.

However, unlike texts by New England female local colorists, which Kaplan claims "negotiate [social identity] conflict in the narrative construction of common ground among classes both to efface and reinscribe social hierarchies,"[43] Chopin's texts imagine such common ground as a vehicle for social advancement for Louisiana peoples of European- and Canadian-French ancestry. Through the acquisition of gentry class values, as well as particular types of and attitudes toward work, Louisiana Creoles and Cajuns become fundamentally like participants in northern white middle-class Anglo-Saxon Protestant culture, even though their coloration, dialect, and religion point to their surfaces of difference.

Thus, Chopin's texts work to assimilate Louisiana Creoles and Cajuns into the dominant culture by preserving them as distinct ethnic categories that nonetheless, through class and gender conformity, are part of the white race.

Werner Sollors's study of the term "ethnicity" shows how its construction as a category of identity is based on the continual deployment of that category as *difference*, or not-ness.[44] Sollors suggests that ethnicity is a negative space in which the ethnic Other is caught in the impossible position of being neither/nor. He quotes the ethnopsychoanalyst Georges Devereux as saying, "If one is nothing but a Spartan, a capitalist, a proletarian, or a Buddhist, one is next door to being nothing and therefore even to not being at all" (qtd. in Sollors 288). Because ethnicity is afforded meaning through its continual *dis*placement, "ethnicity" becomes a floating signifier without a stable referent. As a result, the ethnic Other lives a tenuous existence because she or he is eternally re-presentable.

Kwame Anthony Appiah, like Sollors, suggests that the category "race," too, is given meaning through its negative construction in a relationship based on contrast.[45] But Appiah argues that unlike ethnicity, race's "nothingness" locates a fixed referent through the subsequent transformation of that nothingness into "somethingness." Whereas Appiah makes a useful and necessary distinction between the categories of race and ethnicity, Sollars at one point in his essay conflates these two categories of identity in order to demonstrate how easily — and dangerously — the "floating signifier" can collapse into the "fixed referent." Although Sollors uses the signifier "ethnic" to begin the following passage, we can just as easily substitute "racial" to appreciate both Sollors's and Appiah's points. Sollors writes:

> [Racial] identity . . . "is logically and historically the product of the assertion that 'A is an X because he is not a Y'" — a proposition which makes it remarkably easy to identify Xness. By the same token, the definition of Xs as non-Ys threatens to exaggerate their differences in such a way that if the Xs think of themselves as human, they may therefore consider the Ys as somehow nonhuman. (288)

Giving racial identity the signifier "X," which connotes "X-ness," even if X-ness is originally constructed as being in contrast with Y-ness, gives X an *essence*, a prelinguistic "thingness" in itself that can exist outside the boundaries of the relationship in which it was formed. Thus, even though ethnic identity may be initially constructed as fluid and malleable, it can easily be collapsed into racial identity, which is fixed and unchanging. Race, then, is a totalizing demarcation of identity rooted in *essential difference* and, as such, determines who is assimilable into the cultural mainstream and who is not.

Such an understanding of the fragility of the category "ethnicity" and the irredeemability of the category "race" indicates the urgency of Chopin's fiction to "color" her local Creoles and Cajuns "white" in order to include these European- and Canadian-French peoples in the field of whiteness and thus extend to them social privilege and political entitlement. Whiteness is thus ascertained as a cultural way of being in the world, an adherence to social codes of behavior that mark a person as being essentially like the preferred social group. And the speedy pursuit of that goal was heightened by the question of who deserved the protections of basic human, social, and political rights in so volatile a decade as the 1890s.[46]

Chopin was writing during one of the most violent periods in America's racial history. During the 1890s white vigilante violence, which most often took the form of black lynching, was at an all-time high and "often included torture, burning, dismemberment, and, in the case of black men, ritual castration" (Gunning, *Race* 5). Against this extreme racism, Chopin's local color fiction took a "soft" position on race by endorsing the New South and preaching the New Paternalism, ideals of white mastery wherein former slaveholders cared for their neighbors of color through the honor and duty of noblesse oblige. Likewise, Chopin's free people of color prefer subservience to independence, so long as their masters/employers are of the kindly, new southern mind. Not radically racist, Chopin's fiction nonetheless implicitly accepted arguments of white supremacy and thus negotiated a political position on race relations that historians have come to identify as "conservative."

Both George M. Fredrickson and Joel Williamson's landmark studies on the history of race and racial discourse in America situate racial conservatism as an accommodationist position between abolitionist liberalism on the political left and southern Democratic radicalism on the right.[47] As the dominant northern and southern Republican view on race even

during Reconstruction, conservatism was "softer" on race than radicalism, but nonetheless racist at heart, as indicated by its dangerous engagement with white supremacist rhetoric. Racial conservatism held
that blackness was innately inferior to whiteness and that, as such, black
Americans — like unformed children — were in need of guidance and
protection. With the right nurturing and supervision, so the conservative
argument went, blacks could be angelic followers of the light. However,
the underside of that argument was that, left to their own devices, blacks
were just as likely to return to their "natural" bestial and savage state. This
potential to slip into the radical rhetoric of blacks as uncivilized beasts
marked conservative racial thought as essentially racist; as Williamson
has deftly observed, "the slide from a Conservative to a Radical posture
in race, from a need to see the Negro as angel to a need to see the Negro
as devil, was deeply grooved and well lubricated" (302).

It should come as no surprise, then, that a central tenet of Chopin's
texts is: "'Is you wi'te o' is you black? . . . Dat w'at I wants ter know,'"[48]
especially in a region that "had the highest percentage of mixed-race ancestry of any American city or state. Since New Orleans had a heterogeneous citizenry comprising Italians, Spaniards, and French as well as
blacks and people of mixed race, it was impossible to differentiate people
simply by color or language — free mulattoes, for instance, were usually
French-speaking" (Taylor 4).

Thus, though valued for its mimetic qualities, Chopin's fiction *medi-
ates* for a northern-based periodical press Louisiana's specific, complex
social and racial history. Her fiction's agenda to color local Creoles and
Cajuns white and the necessity of that agenda to occasionally deploy orthodox representations of femininity in its service speaks to the importance of her *Youth's Companion* stories and their role in facilitating our
understanding of the body of her work.

2 Coloring Locals

"For Marse Chouchoute,"
"A Wizard from Gettysburg,"
and "A Rude Awakening"

"For Marse Chouchoute" is notable as Chopin's first piece of short fiction to be accepted by and published in the *Youth's Companion*. Billed on the front page of the 20 August 1891, edition, the story appeared with a subtitle added by the publisher, "For Marse Chouchoute: A Colored Boy's Fidelity." [1] Chopin's local color piece is her first *Companion* story of many to address the change in Louisiana's post-Civil War social order from an antebellum slave society to postbellum emancipation. As such, "For Marse Chouchoute" teaches America's first generation of young white males to reach adolescence since Reconstruction their proper relationship and responsibility to others in society through the inculcation of white, Anglo-Saxon, Protestant middle-class values.

In addition to its compatibility with the *Companion*'s mission, Chopin's first *YC* story can be located historically within a movement operating in Louisiana between roughly the late-1870s and the mid-1890s. That movement has been described by Joseph Tregle as a campaign to mythologize specifically Creoles as exclusive "white" descendants of French and Spanish nobility, the purpose of which was to argue that through noble blood, and thus social class superiority, the Creole deserved recognition as part of America's white middle-to-upper-middle-class hegemony. [2]

Tregle's impressive scholarship details how the necessity for this campaign to declare the Creole white resulted from a slow-but-sure shift in Louisiana's social, political, and economic bases of power during the nineteenth century. After the Louisiana Purchase in 1803, the French and Spanish ruling class's stronghold on Louisiana culture began to erode when large numbers of wealthy, educated Anglo-Americans migrated to the state. This "American" faction developed alongside the formerly hegemonic Spanish-and-French Louisiana populations, and so, in order to strengthen its claim to landholding privileges against the newcomers, this latter group deployed the term "creole" to mean *any native-born* Louisianian in order to emphasize its own "prior rights" as Louisiana born-and-bred citizens.[3]

To say that "Creole" as an identity was convoluted throughout most of the nineteenth century, then, is an understatement. Because any native-born Louisianian could make claim to the title "Creole," the term was used to describe people along the entire spectrum of the color line. "Creole" bespoke no particular social or economic class, either. The term was applied to children of African slaves, both those who remained indigent after the war and the few who became successful and wealthy members of the planter class;[4] it referred to the progeny of Cajuns, both the rural farmers and the plantation masters descended from Canadian refugees fleeing British rule after the French-Indian War; and it referred to Native Americans and people of mixed racial heritage as well.[5]

However, after the Civil War, when the guarantee of at least some position of privilege within America's social hierarchy was lost to the Gallic and Spanish American populations along with a legalized slave system, and, even more critically, during Reconstruction, when northern carpetbag governments enforced the Fourteenth and Fifteenth Amendments in southern regions, Louisiana's "white" French and Spanish American population set into motion the fiction that the term "Creole" only ever referred to those (white) Louisiana residents of pure Gallic or Spanish descent. Because Louisiana's formerly legalized tri-caste system of white / free colored / slave had been abolished, people of virtually all shades on the color line engaged in a frantic claim to "whiteness" to guarantee their social preferment and political entitlement as a new, culturally instituted dual-caste system of white / black began to emerge.[6] The sometimes darker features of people of French and Spanish origins, as well as the hidden truth of the region's mixed-heritage population, intensified the campaign to construct the Creole as a white ethnic category distinguishable from the black race.

As an heir to the first decade of crusaders in the campaign to declare the Creole white, Chopin reinforces the work of these pioneers in her texts.[7] Making sure her texts perform the work of marking particularly the economically disempowered Creoles as biologically white,[8] Chopin further "whitens" her Creole characters socially by acculturating them to Wasp middle-class norms. As her first *Companion* text in this tradition, "For Marse Chouchoute" is a particularly didactic tale. Chopin teaches her moral of Creole acculturation through Armand "Chouchoute" Verchette, a fatherless, economically (and thus socially) disempowered sixteen-year-old Creole who promises to turn around his and his sick mother's fortunes when he gains employment as a mail-carrying horseman for the Cloutierville Post Office. Chouchoute's chances at economic advancement and social mobility are threatened, however, when he indulges in his Creole culture's practice of "ball dancing" (often performed in rural cabins) while he is on company time. However, thanks to his worshipping comrade, Wash, an African American boy who is "idealized . . . as legally free, [but] emotionally enslaved" (Starke 29) to his white "Marse," or Master, Chouchoute's professional obligations are fulfilled and his opportunity for upward mobility preserved.

Chopin's idealization of Wash as the eminently good and faithful servant echoes Harriet Beecher Stowe's treatment of the character Uncle Tom in *Uncle Tom's Cabin*. Like Stowe in her treatment of Uncle Tom, Chopin exhibits sympathetic racial inclinations when she dramatizes Wash as the harder-working, morally superior foil to Chouchoute. However, Chopin (like Stowe) nonetheless racializes her character when she attributes to him certain, immutable traits that are essentially different from a hegemonic white, Anglo-Saxon Protestant standard. Regardless of whether Chopin articulates Wash's precultural essence as perfection or dereliction, then, the act of racializing him nonetheless constructs his essential difference; it hails into being the very category of race, in the first place. Thus, whether an author intends them to or not, racial articulations inevitably give way to racist ones because black, as a category, can materialize only as a distinction against white, the standard, central norm against which racial difference in the nineteenth century was constructed.[9]

Consequently, we should not be surprised at the end of the tale when Chopin sacrifices Wash, her representation of essential (black) perfection, for the benefit of teaching Chouchoute a lesson. While Chouchoute dances at the ball, oblivious to his deadlines, Wash remains ever mindful of his "marse's" responsibilities. Wash thus "rescues" Chouchoute by dashing to the Cloutierville train station on Chouchoute's horse to meet the incoming locomotive. Although Wash successfully delivers the mail on time, in a cruel turn of events he is thrown by Chouchoute's horse and suffers fatal injuries. When Chouchoute learns of Wash's accident and impending death, he arrives at the station tearful and grief stricken, ignorantly pleading "'O Wash, Wash! W'at made you, Wash?'" Characteristic of the literary type of the idealized Negro, Wash's reply focuses on Chouchoute's welfare rather than his own, and his fateful words end the story: "'You ain't mad? . . . I boun' to git well, 'ca'se who — gwine — watch Marse — Chouchoute?'" (*CW* 110).

The rhetorical answer to Wash's question, "no one," indicates the problem Chopin allows her *Companion* readers to consider for a new generation of white southern males, a generation that could not count on the advantages a slave system of free black labor might have afforded. For the post-Reconstruction era in which Chopin was writing was a time in which formerly slaveholding southerners were forced to seek "an alternate route for white development" (Gunning, "Kate Chopin" 72). The various titles assigned to this text by Chopin and her publisher, then, become relevant here, as do the separate readings these titles suggest. By adding a subtitle, the *Companion*'s title for Chopin's text lends itself to being read as Wash's dedication to his white master: "A Colored Boy's Fidelity for Marse Chouchoute." However, Chopin herself simply wrote the title as "For Marse Chouchoute," a title that suggests she dedicated the story to the Creole boy, the one main character left in the end to inherit Chopin's parable.

Chopin's text suggests that in postbellum America, white folks' alternate route to development will entail not only the personal dedication, ambition, and responsibility of the Protestant work ethic — a moral near and dear to the *Companion*'s heart — but also a reformed style of white management over people of color. As Henry W. Grady, the man who coined the term "New South," wrote, the New South's masters must rule not by "the cowardly menace of mask or shot-gun, but [by] the peaceful majesty of intelligence and responsibility" (quoted in Gunning, *Race* 122). In *The New South*, Grady imagined a kinder white "mastery" of southern blacks, which absolved white southerners of the sins of slavery but nonetheless allowed them to maintain a racially stratified, antebellum social order under the post-Reconstruction political regime.

As a *Companion* story, "For Marse Chouchoute" is instructive in this vein. Throughout Chopin's text, Chouchoute does not fit the mold of Grady's new southern master. His internal character flaws that contribute to the story's ending — his arrogance, irresponsibility, and complacency — are first indicated by his response to the Cloutierville postmaster's speech, which opens the text: "'An' now, young man, w'at you want to remember is this — an' take it fer yo' motto: "No monkey-shines with Uncle Sam." You undastan'? You aware now o' the penalties attached to monkey-shinin' with Uncle Sam. I reckon that's 'bout all I got to say; so you be on han' promp' tomorrow mornin' at seven o'clock, to take charge o' the United States mail-bag'" (*CW* 104).

Chopin brands Chouchoute "exotic" at his very introduction when she describes his reaction to this portentous oration. "Armand — or Chouchoute, as every one chose to call him, following the habit of the Creoles in giving nicknames — had listened a little impatiently." Self-conscious of the fact that the northern periodical press for whom she was writing was not familiar with the Creole culture to which Chouchoute belonged, Chopin explains that (foreign) culture and its practices while she simultaneously distances herself from them.[10] Her authorial positioning of superiority to Chouchoute and her alignment with the northern editors and their imagined readership are indicated by the little aside the narrator whispers in between the dashes: " — or Chouchoute, as every one chose to call him, following the habit of the Creoles in giving nicknames —." This kind of confidence establishes a common bond of identity between the narrator and reader that Chouchoute does not share. Chopin's authorial stance thus establishes her authorization to eventually reprimand Chouchoute, to shake a disapproving moral finger at him at the story's end, and to set her text up to function as a sharp warning to all young, white males who find themselves in a position like Chouchoute's.

However, although Chouchoute's ability to serve as the reformed southern master remains in question, his biological right to do so does not. Chouchoute's superiority of race is ensured through the figure of his mother, whose own ghostly white and frail body symbolically protects Chouchoute's cultural inheritance of privilege as a white male. Madame Verchette's "white and wasted hand which she rested upon the boy's black curls" (*CW* 105) guarantees her dark-haired son's claim to irreproachable whiteness through both its color and its bodily resemblance to the cultural ideal of southern femininity (Jones 3–50). Because Madame Verchette's illness renders her whiteness overblown, her purity (of race and character) is confirmed not only by her deathly pallor but also her passivity, idleness, and asexuality. Such absolute goodness, validated by the attainment of other revered feminine qualities, is further illustrated by her beloved status within the community and church: "Every one was kind to Madame Verchette. Neighbors ran in of mornings to help her with her work — she could do so little for herself. And often the good priest, Père Antoine, came to sit with her and talk innocent gossip" (*CW* 105).

Although Madame's Catholicism distinguishes her from a hegemonic "American" Anglo-Saxon Protestant population, her unquestionable whiteness unequivocally bespeaks her "not blackness." Thus, by marking her essential difference from blackness and her religious distinction from Protestantism, Chopin constructs Madame Verchette's Creolism as a category of ethnicity that is nonetheless part of the white race.

Scholars of southern history have long noted that the tremendous symbolic importance of the white female body to southern racial ideology lay in its capacity to shore up an entire southern way of life.[11] The white man's superiority of gender and race was always argued, historically, in defense of virtuous white womanhood. Just as the rape of black female slaves by white masters in antebellum years was condoned as the preservation of the white mistress's purity, so the (white) lynching of potential black male rapists in postbellum years was argued in defense of virtuous white womanhood.

The (black) rape of white women, that imagined threat of black male desire, confirmed the desirable value of white female purity, while it simultaneously threatened to undo that purity through violent means.[12] However, in Chopin's story, Madame Verchette's integrity is not held in place through the threat of black male desire but rather through the heavily romanticized lens of black male adoration in the character of Wash: "To say that Wash was fond of Madame Verchette and her son is to be poor in language to express devotion. He worshipped her as if she were already an angel in Paradise" (*CW* 105).

Chopin's description of Madame Verchette as the soon-to-be "angel in Paradise" evokes the language of British poet Coventry Patmore, whose midcentury poem "The Angel in the House" advocated woman's role as nurturer of the domestic and, by extension, savior of the worldly sphere (Gilbert and Gubar, *Anthology* 168). Although Patmore's poem was emblematic of the mid-nineteenth-century British cultural construction of white middle-class domestic femininity, similar discursive constructs circulated in America during the same period.[13] Chopin's reconfiguration of the white female body from sexual to religious object through the lens of the black male gaze serves to ensure Madame Verchette's objectification as a transcendental signifier of female virtue, as well as Wash's idealized alignment with a dominant white social order that was held in place through its reverence for white women.

It is in these heavily romanticized moments during which Chopin renders her African American character a willing participant in a culture of white dominance that she ultimately reveals her nostalgic attachment to the Old South and both mourns and warns of the passing of a previous "grand society." Thus, although Chopin separates herself from a radically racist tradition of literature that circulated pejorative representations of African Americans, she ultimately alters those racial stereotypes only as a means toward condemning the Old South's violence against blacks as a problem of methods rather than purpose.

This "soft" but nonetheless white supremacist position on the Race Question marks Chopin as a racial conservative in a time of fervent racial radicalism. Chopin's "conservative racism," which emerges through her romanticization of Wash, can be seen when we compare her contrasting uplifted and pejorative representations of the African American character. When Chopin opens her text with the postmaster's speech, for instance, it is Wash whom she aligns with the (northern) Uncle Sam of whom the postmaster speaks. Wash, the idealized black patriot, whose own name echoes his connection with the Union's white forefathers, respects the voice of national authority and takes all too seriously the consequences of monkey-shinin' with Uncle Sam. Wash "had listened with the deepest respect and awe to every word of the rambling admonition. . . . He felt, too, deeply conscious of the great weight of responsibility which this new office brought with it" (*CW* 104–5).

Not so Chouchoute, whose impatience with his (northern) superior and whose (southern) arrogance toward Wash indicates he has not yet achieved the self-mastery necessary to be master of his postbellum world. Flaunting his position of cultural superiority, Chouchoute taunts, "'W'y, I'm goin' to git thirty dolla' a month, Wash; w'at you say to that? Betta 'an hoein' cotton, ain't it?' He laughed with a triumphant ring in his voice" (*CW* 104). Chouchoute's cruel reminder of the itinerant jobs available to Wash even after Reconstruction further articulates the contrast between Wash's and Chouchoute's racial identities via slave labor versus salaried work. Yet, because of Chouchoute's arrogance, Chopin indicates he has not yet achieved the restraint or intelligence necessary to accommodate the New South's reformed treatment of blacks. Now a mere salaried worker in subordination to management and Uncle Sam, Chouchoute can be among the New South's masters only when he learns to make racial subordination invisible and thereby (ostensibly) more compassionate.

Although she idealizes Wash as the quick-thinking, quick-acting, more responsible being, Chopin still insists on reminding readers of his culturally inferior place. Unlike other romantic literary portrayals of African Americans in the nineteenth century, Chopin does not use external beauty to mirror her character's internal goodness.[14] Rather, Chopin employs her characters' physical appearances as external markers of difference that signify their cultural place within the social hierarchy. Whereas Wash "was very black, and slightly deformed; a small boy, scarcely reaching to the shoulder of his companion . . . Chouchoute was tall for his sixteen years, and carried himself well" (*CW* 104). Her attitude toward the two is further demonstrated by the following description:

Chouchoute was a delightful young fellow; no one could help loving him. His heart was as warm and cheery as his own southern sunbeams. If he was born with an unlucky trick of forgetfulness — or better, thoughtlessness — no one ever felt much like blaming him for it, so much did it seem a part of his happy, careless nature. And why was that faithful watch-dog, Wash, always at Marse Chouchoute's heels, if it were not to be hands and ears and eyes to him, more than half the time? (*CW* 105)

Chopin's alternate portrayals of both Chouchoute and Wash in this passage work to solidify already established ethnic and racial stereotypes, while they also address those categories' hierarchical placement within southern Louisiana society. Engaging with the essentialist language of biological determinism, Chopin writes that Chouchoute "was born with an unlucky trick of forgetfulness — or better, thoughtlessness . . . so much did it seem a part of his happy, careless nature." Drawn this way, Chouchoute's irresponsibility registers simply the underside of his Creole fun-loving whimsicality, making him a flawed, but nonetheless *fully human* being, and lovingly so.[15] Hence, Chopin preserves the Creole as an ethnic category while she simultaneously reinscribes its, and by extension Chouchoute's, legitimate claim to whiteness.

Chopin's representation of Chouchoute here stands in stark contrast to her portrayal of Wash, who, through a rhetorical sleight of hand, is transformed from human to animal, significantly a watchdog whose natural, inevitable role (echoing the argument for slavery) is to serve his master. Wash's subhuman characterization is reinforced with other objectified representations of African Americans throughout the text, particularly those onlookers at Gros-Léon's ball. Denied entrance because of their race, these male onlookers are described in audiovisual terms: "At the windows appeared the dusky faces of negroes, their bright eyes gleaming as they viewed the scene within and mingled their loud guffaws with the medley of sound that was already deafening" (*CW* 106).

While the men in this scene are looking at the dancers, what Chopin constructs for the reader's view is the spectacle of the men themselves. Objectified as bodily parts, the "dusky faces" and "bright eyes" are not seen through, but rather looked at, as if they were specimens behind glass. Furthermore, the men are granted only limited access to language, since, mingled with the overwhelming din of the ball, their undecipherable words are rendered inarticulate.

Significantly, it is language — that all-powerful attribute of humanity that Chopin denies to the onlookers at Gros-Léon's ball — that she permits Wash access to at the story's end. In his only monologue of the text, Wash, on his deathbed, explains to Chouchoute his selfless rationale for delivering the U.S. mail, which gave way to the heroic act that will ultimately end his life:

"Marse Chouchoute," the boy whispered, so low that no one could hear him but his friend, "I was gwine 'long de big road, pas' Marse Gros-Léon's, an' I seed Spunky tied dah wid de mail. Dar warn't a minute — I 'clar', Marse Chouchoute, dar warn't a minute — to fotch you. W'at makes my head tu'n 'roun' dat away?"

"Neva mine, Wash; keep still; don't you try to talk," entreated Chouchoute.

"You ain't mad, Marse Chouchoute?"

The lad could only answer with a hand pressure.

"Dar warn't a minute, so I gits top o' Spunky — I neva seed nuttin' cl'ar de road like dat. I come 'long side — de train — an' fling de sack. I seed 'im kotch it, and I don' know nuttin' mo' 'cep' mis'ry, tell I see you — a-comin' frough de do'. Mebby Ma'ame Verchette know some'pin," he murmured faintly, " 'w'at gwine make my — head quit tu'nin' 'round dat away. I boun' to git well, 'ca'se who — gwine — watch Marse — Chouchoute?" (*CW* 110)

The dying Wash's self-sacrificing concern for his "Marse," Chouchoute, instead of himself in this passage is nothing short of pathetic. Readers trained in sentimental fiction could not have helped but mourn Wash's impending death because of its abject injustice. And so Chopin's authorial rebuke is aimed at Chouchoute, who, as the text indicates, is largely to blame. Wash's black dialect, much farther afield from standard English than Chouchoute's colloquial southern drawl, indicates his inferiority, which, when coupled with his romanticized portrayal as absolute-goodness-that-blinds-judgement, seals his fate as a perpetual dependent who requires adult protection. Chopin's text, then, takes Chouchoute to task for not properly safeguarding, or in the language of the New South, "managing," his essentially inferior charge. To borrow Sandra Gunning's words regarding another Chopin text, "Racial [mistreatment] is accounted for as simply a . . . problem of Creole arrogance out-of-bounds. . . . So, the story implies [inhumanity] will disappear upon [Chouchoute's personal reform] rather than with a reform of black and white power relations."[16] Rather than critique a social hierarchy based on race, "For Marse Chouchoute" warns readers of the tragedies that will occur if the upcoming generation of white males does not learn how to maintain that hierarchy through responsible, gentle/manly means.

"A WIZARD FROM GETTYSBURG"

"A Wizard from Gettysburg" takes up where "For Marse Chouchoute" leaves off, as it is a story about the spoils of war and the need to regenerate the war-ravaged South.[17] Bertrand Delmandé, a white Creole teenager of the postbellum era, is Chopin's model of the kind of masculinity that will enable white male supremacy to prosper in the New South. As Chopin's second story to be published in the *Companion*, "A Wizard from Gettysburg" is unlike its predecessor in that it more readily assumes readers' understanding of the Creoles as white and explicitly attributes the Delmandés' declining fortune to the devastating effects of the war.

Also unlike "For Marse Chouchoute," "A Wizard from Gettysburg" recognizes that the rhetorical construct of "gentle/manliness," or the recasting of the prewar's powerful Master as the postwar's gentle father, is not enough to maintain white supremacy in a new social order. "A Wizard from Gettysburg" mourns the loss of the Old South's economic strength and thus seeks to preserve white male privilege through financial means. It accomplishes this goal by steering young white males toward professionalism, a newly available avenue of success that transforms the (sentimentalized) gentle/man into the *genteel man* whose formal cultural and educational training ensure continued white male prosperity in the South's changing social and economic climate.[18]

Endorsing an economically empowered, genteel masculinity for the New South works to not only preserve white male privilege but also defend the elevated social position of the defeated antebellum slave-owning master, whose former economic strength provided the resources for sons to succeed their fathers as community leaders. Partly because the subordination of women and people of color to the white male master constituted the structural underpinnings of the southern slave economy; partly because race subordination in particular remained the white male's ideological tool for continued supremacy in a new, theoretically egalitarian society; and partly because the plantation remained the primary unit of economic production in the South even after the war (so that the plantation still operated as a self-contained, microcosmic government), the social hierarchy of woman's subordination to man and blacks' subordination to whites continued to hold currency in the region well into the twentieth century.[19]

In order to justify the supremacy of the white male, which required the continued stratification of people according to gender and race even after the war, white supremacist activists often turned to religious discourse for authoritative support. Pastor Benjamin Morgan Palmer, a New Orleans Presbyterian minister, was just one accommodating clergyman whose writings were notorious for advocating the father's power within the structure of the family unit. Treating the family itself as a transitive semiotic body through which the Biblical representation of God the Father passed, Palmer's rhetoric also transformed the family into a model for governing society as a whole. One of Palmer's influential pamphlets, written during Reconstruction in 1876, at once both depicts the family unit as mirror of divine arrangement and transforms it into a social ruling body. Eugene Genovese quotes Palmer as having written:

> "In this little empire [of the family], the parent is supreme, and no appeal can lie to a higher tribunal, except the divine. The power to enforce is as complete as the authority is absolute. It is a government under which the subjects are helpless. . . . Under every government, the sovereignty must rest in some recognized head; there must be a last tribunal, beyond which no appeal can lie."
>
> In the family, the fundamental unit on which state and church rest, the power of God, "attaches to the husband and father." (qtd. in Genovese 69–70)

Thus, the importance of maintaining the father as the family figurehead was to preserve not only a financial economy but also an economy of race and gender relations that valued the white male patriarch, an economy that underpinned the entire operation of southern life.

The impact of such race and gender ideology on the southern consciousness is registered in "A Wizard from Gettysburg," a story that conflates regional prosperity with patriarchal vitality. Chopin represents the South as a distinct and gendered body in this story by situating the region's deteriorated postbellum state in the figure of Bertrand Delmandé, an aged, mentally feeble, homeless Creole Confederate soldier who, when he finally stumbles back to his home state of Louisiana, is mistaken by his relatives for a tramp. Delmandé's grandson, the third in a line of sons to bear the family name of Bertrand Delmandé, fails to identify the Gettysburg war veteran as his grandfather, even though the senior Delmandé curiously knows details about the family's Bon-Accueil plantation. Although the elder Delmandé reveals his identity to the family-at-large at the story's end, the possibility of his resuming his function as the family patriarch disintegrates when he quickly regresses to a state of dementia. Thus, even though his genius and foresight rescue his progeny and validate the integrity of his former way of life, they cannot return him or the Old South to the state they were in prior to the war.

Although bittersweet, Chopin's ending nonetheless justifies the absolute power invested in antebellum masters by portraying the elder Delmandé as the "wizard" who restores privilege to the next generation of his patrilineal line. Arriving on the plantation just in time to learn that his grandson will not attend medical school as planned because the war has depleted the family fortune, the elder Delmandé renews his family's economic solvency by unearthing a pot of gold he had buried before marching off to battle. Although this quasi-magical act reinstates Delmandé as the family's provider (a discursive move that promotes the mythical grandeur of the Old South), its efficacy is only temporary. Only seconds after he has lucidly reunited himself with his family, the bedraggled soldier's dementia immediately returns. "Madame," he says, addressing his wife as a stranger, "an old soldier, wounded on the field of Gettysburg, craves for himself and his two little children your kind hospitality" (*CW* 130).

Because the construct of the antebellum patriarch is dead, Chopin resurrects it in Delmandé as a mere specter of manhood, a liminal figure between genius and insanity; the extraordinary and the ordinary; even life and death. Delmandé's dementia, mingled with potential senility and amnesia, all operate in tandem with Chopin's metaphor of wizardry featured in her title; mental disease registers the underside of exceptional mental ability in this fiction. Not only does Delmandé foretell the financial casualties of war by hiding gold instead of paper currency that could lose its value, he also procures the education his grandson needs to enter medical school. Through the metaphor of wizardry, the Old South is quite literally resurrected in Delmandé, and its lost dignity is restored when Delmandé's performance in the context of family relations enables the continuation of the privileged white male line.

In one sense, then, Chopin's story simply enacts a twist on the old Oedipal drama. Instead of the son killing off the father, the father steps down to make way for the son. The (grand)father of Chopin's fiction is secure in abdicating his authority because he is assured of his place in the social hierarchy. Instead of worrying about competition from younger sons, he can expect submission and deference. These ideas have their roots in colonial concepts of masculinity, which, because of the agrarian architecture of plantation life, did not lose their potency in the South as they did in the industrialized North or the expansionist West.[20] In his investigation into configurations of masculinity in colonial times, Anthony Rotundo explains that while "a person's identity was bound up in the performance of social roles, not in the expression of self," men in particular "were judged by their contribution to the larger community." Thus,

a man's "publick usefulness" was a crucial measure of his worth. Men who carried out their duties to family and community were men to admire.

The performance of social obligation often required a man to act against his own will. To carry out such obligations, a man had to learn submission to superiors, to fate, to duty itself. . . . So young people deferred to old, sons yielded to fathers, women submitted to men, and men of all ages acquiesced in their social responsibilities. Moreover, society was arranged by class as well as age and gender. People of the upper orders expected their inferiors to defer to them, so a man bowed to his superiors just as he submitted to God's will. (13)

As the earlier example of Pastor Palmer's book illustrates, these ideas were reworked in late nineteenth-century rhetoric to conflate the familial father with God, so that, by the time a young male assumed the roles of husband and father, there were no more superiors to whom he need answer. However, in order for this configuration of power to work, the rest of the community had to submit to the hierarchical pecking order. Thus, unmarried sons, though heirs apparent to the family throne, were expected to yield to their fathers.

In "A Wizard from Gettysburg," the youngest Bertrand Delmandé not only honors this revered tradition of masculinity, he also embodies the reformed white master coming of age just in time to rule the New South. Chopin strategically places the grandson Delmandé on the threshold of manhood in terms of his age, drawing him as "a fine, bright-looking boy of fourteen years, — fifteen, perhaps" (CW 124). Fourteen or fifteen, it doesn't matter; the significance here is that Bertrand is about to enter gendered adulthood and, by doing so, represents the new and upcoming generation of white males born after Reconstruction.

Bertrand's very first encounter with a white male elder in the story demonstrates his respect for elders required of a previous generation, as well as the noblesse oblige required of the new. When he stumbles upon his (unidentified) grandfather just beyond the plantation gates, Bertrand plays both the roles of respectful son and Christian philanthropist:

> The pony started suddenly and violently at something there in the turn of the road, and just under the hedge. It looked like a bundle of rags at first. But it was a tramp, seated upon a broad, flat stone.
>
> Bertrand had no maudlin consideration for tramps as a species; he had only that morning driven from the place one who was making himself unpleasant at the kitchen window.
>
> But this tramp was old and feeble. His beard was long, and as white as new-ginned cotton, and when Bertrand saw him he was engaged in stanching a wound in his bare heel with a fistful of matted grass.
>
> "What's wrong, old man?" asked the boy, kindly. (CW 124–25)

As the antebellum male enmeshed in the web of community and family hierarchies, Bertrand is considerate of his elders; as the gentle/man of the New South, he is compassionate and willing to care for those less fortunate than he.

Furthermore, by electing to enter one of the rising professions, Bertrand rides the new trend of masculine success by choosing to study medicine, a field moving toward professionalized status in the late 1800s. Again, Bertrand's "contemporary" masculinity is reconciled with the old when his career choice is not made by him individually but rather as a result of family negotiations.[21] Chopin's use of the passive voice in the following passage indicates just how collaborative a decision Bertrand's choice of career was. Upon seeing the tramp's wound, Bertrand thinks, "since *it's decided* that I'm to be a physician some day, I can't begin to practice too early" [emphasis added] (*CW* 125).

The importance of combining noblesse oblige with a social hierarchizing of white males that respects age is indicated by Bertrand's decision to help this particular tramp, and not another. Chopin writes that Bertrand had "no maudlin consideration for tramps as a species; he had only that morning driven from the place one who was making himself unpleasant at the kitchen window." But Bertrand chose to take pity on *this particular tramp* precisely because he was "old and feeble."

Such a fictionalized scenario of the bourgeois white Creole helping the disempowered white tramp performs yet another important task: It imagines the dissolution of economic class stratification among whites, a move that both encourages solidarity among whites and inevitably excludes blacks. The importance of white class solidarity to the systematic oppression of blacks is explained by one of Chopin's contemporaries, Thomas Dixon. In his novel *The Leopard's Spots*, Dixon wrote: "In a moment the white race [would be] fused into a homogeneous mass of love, sympathy, hate, and revenge. The rich and the poor, the learned and the ignorant, the banker and the blacksmith, the great and the small, they [would all be] one now" (qtd. in Gunning, *Race* 40).

However, as historian Robert Wiebe has noted, white class solidarity was itself a myth that was only deployed by the (white) middle class when it suited their immediate interests. Wiebe observes that "only the poorer Southern whites had reason to doubt the serviceability of the color line. Often struggling in a net of mortgages, agricultural ignorance, and erratic prices, they had no guarantee of a lasting advantage over anyone (58–59)."

Thus, economically disempowered southern whites jockeyed for position with southern blacks because, even with the privilege of being white, they were usually unable to participate in the myth of upward mobility and lift themselves above the dredges of a stereotypical black economic, social, and material lifestyle.[22]

The elder Bertrand Delmandé, as we meet him in the beginning of the story, belongs to this category of indigent southern whites. Old, bedraggled, and injured, the elder Delmandé's body signifies both his regionally displaced and locally homeless status within the community. His homelessness in particular emphasizes his loss of privilege and authority because, without connection to lineage and stripped of his former position as head of the household, he is without the vestiges of power and virility that typically established a male as a "man" in the late-nineteenth-century South.

Thus, only by ignoring the hierarchy of class can the younger Bertrand allow the tramp to tread on his family's property. However, the subversive danger in such an act is this: By bringing the tramp onto the plantation and allowing him access to spaces typically occupied by residents there, the (lower-class) tramp threatens to unsettle the existing hierarchy of race by symbolically displacing people with positions of authority inside the family. Chopin vocalizes such danger through 'Cindy, the African American house matron whose status below the Delmandé family, but uncertain in regard to the tramp, is threatened by such a social shake-up. 'Cindy witnesses the younger Bertrand leading his yet-unidentified grandfather into the yard astride Picayune:

> "W'at's dat you's bringin' in dis yard, boy? top dat hoss?"
>
> She received no reply. Bertrand, indeed, took no notice of her inquiry.
>
> "Fu' a boy w'at goes to school like you does — whar's yo' sense?" she went on, with a fine show of indignation; then, muttering to herself,
>
> "Ma'ame Bertrand an' Marse St. Ange ain't gwine stan' dat, I knows dey ain't. Dah! ef he ain't done sot 'im on de gall'ry, plumb down in his pa's rockin'-cheer!"
>
> Which the boy had done; seated the tramp in a pleasant corner of the veranda, while he went in search of bandages for his wound. (*CW* 125)

"In his Pa's Rockin-cheer"

Illustration for "A Wizard from Gettysburg" printed in the *Youth's Companion,*
New England edition, *The American Periodical Series on Microfilm,* 7 July 1892,
page 346. Image published with permission of ProQuest Information and
Learning Company. Further reproduction is prohibited without permission.

By placing the tramp in his father's rocking chair on the gallery and searching in his grandmother's closet for bandages, the younger Bertrand allows the (perceived) outsider to trespass on sanctified familial spaces. While 'Cindy appeals to Bertrand's identity as a young scholar to rectify his betrayal of the "common sense" of family hierarchy, Bertrand remains oblivious to such "intellectual" transgressions. The racial ideology that so privileges Bertrand remains invisible to him, just as that same ideology, which has severe material consequences for 'Cindy, is quite visible to her.

'Cindy's worry that *she* is the one made vulnerable by white class reformation is justified when she articulates just how fragile her superior footing of family position is when laid against the backdrop of racial prejudice. Arguing that, even though she has proven herself a trustworthy servant, her blackness still has the potential to brand her as a thief and criminal, 'Cindy says to the young Bertrand:

> "You want to listen to me; you gwine git shed o' dat tramp settin' dah naxt to de dinin'-room! W'en de silva be missin', 'tain' you w'at gwine git blame, it's me."
>
> "The silver? Nonsense, 'Cindy; the man's wounded, and can't you see he's out of his head?"
>
> "No mo' outen his head 'an I is. 'Tain' me w'at want to tres' [trust] 'im wid de sto'-room key, ef he is outen his head," she concluded with a disdainful shrug. (*CW* 126)

'Cindy's reasoning regarding the tramp's role in determining her own security of position is sound. As a lucid, homeless wanderer in need of resources, the tramp is not to be trusted; as a madman, he's not to be trusted, either.

But when grandfather Delmandé sheds his tramp image to reveal his "wizardly" capacity, it is the (former) tramp who now worries about the Negroes' thievery, indicating that the younger Bertrand was correct in his gestures of respect toward elders and Christian philanthropy. About to lead his grandson to the buried treasure, the elder Delmandé urges, "Come. Don't let them hear you. Don't let the negroes see us. Get a spade — the little spade that Buck Williams was digging his cistern with" (*CW* 128).

Once himself a thievish threat, grandfather Delmandé, the bearer of fortune, now justifiably fears the thievery of black Others.

Wizardly though he is in restoring fortune to the Delmandé family name, however, the grandfather Delmandé cannot fully restore either himself or the Old South to the state each was in prior to the war. Chopin's ending is as sad and permanent as the closing of a casket, for, even with all of grandfather Delmandé's wisdom and foreknowledge, his dementia stands as an unforgiving reminder of the irreversible spoils of war. However, deep in Chopin's story there lives the promise that the power of the white southern patrician can rise again. Because of the wizard's magical qualities, Chopin's fiction suggests that the grand, dying generation of southern patriarchs provided well enough for their offspring that the new generation can triumph in spite of the North's damage to the southern body politic. "A Wizard from Gettysburg" stands as testimony to *Companion* readers that, even though the Old South's former way of life is gone, its legacy of white supremacy can endure.

"A RUDE AWAKENING"

On 2 February 1893, the *Youth's Companion* published its third short story by Kate Chopin, "A Rude Awakening." The story details how the Bordons, a poor Cajun family living in rural postbellum Louisiana, triumphantly and harmoniously integrate themselves into hegemonic white American culture. Even though Chopin never specifies the Bordon family's ethnic origins in her text, the father's working-class status, the daughter's brown skin and curly black hair, and all of their speech, a nonstandard dialect combining French vocabulary and sentence structure with regional black English, ultimately code them as Cajun. However, Chopin's text is less concerned with what the Bordons specifically are than with what they are not in terms of both ethnicity and race. Although they are not ethnically Creole like the nearby wealthy planter Joe Duplan, they are also decidedly — and significantly — not racially black.

Such racial designation in Chopin's text is catalyzed by the particular presence of one of the Bordons' many black neighbors, Aunt Minty, whose appearances, although infrequent, nonetheless advance the central themes of the tale. When Sylveste Bordon, the family's father, accepts work as a plantation field hand, Aunt Minty witnesses the transformation of his daughter, seventeen-year-old Lolotte, from a member of her own poverty-stricken underclass to the picture of middle-class white femininity. Consider Aunt Minty's reaction when she comes on Lolotte dressed all in white and sitting demurely in the affluent Duplans' drawing room:

> "An' dah you is!" almost shouted aunt Minty, whose black face gleamed in the doorway; "dah you is, settin' down, lookin' jis' like w'ite folks!"
>
> "Ain't I always was w'ite folks, Aunt Mint?" smiled Lolotte, feebly. (*CW* 144)

The rhetorical answer to Lolotte's question — that, no, she is not unequivocally marked as white prior to this point in the text — foregrounds the central dilemma of Chopin's fiction and points to the ideological work it ultimately performs. In the world of Chopin's text, just as in the world of Chopin's lived experiences, the brown-skinned, underprivileged Lolotte has the potential to be read as black until and unless she and her father adhere to bourgeois gender norms. Capitalizing on the inadequacy of external signs to determine one's race definitively, Chopin's text deploys whiteness as a signifier of racial identity whose empirical validity cannot be determined by location on the color line. Rather, whiteness is more readily recognized as a cultural way of being in the world, an adherence to social codes of behavior that are consistent with dominant standards of class and gender.

Thus, Lolotte and Sylveste's subscription to orthodox ideals of middle-class femininity and masculinity allow the Bordon family members to ascend the postbellum cultural ladder, an ascent that marks them as white. However, such social mobility to a racially preferred status is denied the authorially black Aunt Minty, whose cultural positioning remains static throughout the text. The moral of Chopin's tale, then, has to do not only with acculturation but also with access and entry. It bespeaks Cajun assimilability into hegemonic white middle-class American culture, while concomitantly reinscribing African exclusion from such cultural entitlement.

"A Rude Awakening" is Chopin's first *Companion* text to construct the Cajun as a white ethnic category of American identity.[23] Historically, Cajuns differed from the European French in Louisiana in that they came there years after having settled in the former French colony of Acadia in what is now Canada. Although some Louisiana Cajuns rose to the coveted level of planter class, others kept the rural farming lifestyles of their ancestors. Acadians of all economic levels engendered children with African Americans, Native Americans, European Americans, Anglo Americans, and immigrants who entered the state through the port city of New Orleans. Thus, "Cajun" had as tangled a discursive history by Chopin's day as did "Creole," and perhaps even more so, since first-generation Cajun Americans also legitimately made claim to Creole identity as native-born Louisianians.

Not just in her *Companion* stories but throughout her fiction, Chopin articulates Cajuns as the economic underclass of Louisiana society whose whiteness is more or less discernible based on characters' subscription to middle-class codes of behavior. For women, those codes apply to female social and sexual mores;[24] for men, they apply to correct attitudes toward work. From plantation owner, to hireling field hand, to indigent good-for-nothing, Chopin distinguishes male Cajuns from Creoles by their relationships to each other via *work*. Often, planter-class Creoles act as benefactors who introduce their less fortunate Cajun "cousins" to bourgeois morality and comfort.

However, as Chopin's first *Companion* text to code the Cajun as white, "A Rude Awakening" capitalizes on what Chopin assumes to be her readers' confusion over Cajun identity. Indeed, deciphering Chopin's ethnic and racial codification is critical to our ability to make sense of a story such as "A Rude Awakening," whose punch-line ending is predicated upon readers' inability to interpret the Cajun's racial identity. The very plot of "A Rude Awakening" operates through a narrative strategy of deferment, whereby the reader learns the Bordons' racial identity only in a surprise ending that constitutes one of the many "awakenings" in the text.[25] Chopin deliberately prolongs revealing this information by articulating how the members of the Bordon family are variously like and unlike their black neighbors. For instance, even though Sylveste Bordon, the family's father, may not be described in terms of color, we know that his living conditions mirror those of his rural black neighbors, and his speech shares much with what Chopin represents as black dialect.

Moreover, Sylveste harbors an aversion to steady work, a stereotype so commonly applied to African Americans throughout the nineteenth century that it hardly requires mention. These poor work habits, combined with what borders on complete indifference toward his family's well-being, make clear that Sylveste has not been the male provider so central to traditional southern models of the family.[26] Finally, however, fearing that his indolence may have caused the death of his daughter, Lolotte, Sylveste reforms his erring ways and accepts a steady job as a field hand for the Creole planter, Joe Duplan. Sylveste so exaggerates his patriarchal duties that he becomes a virtual zealot, plowing Duplan's fields night and day until "the negroes began to whisper hints of demoniacal possession" (*CW* 142). By assuming the role of the male provider, Sylveste proves his ability to adapt to a system that, for men, produces whiteness through work.

However, as in other of Chopin's fictions about white legitimacy in the South, the veracity of the Bordon family's claim to racial purity ultimately rests on the figure of the white female body. The story of Sylveste Bordon's figurative awakening to the responsibilities of manhood (the most obvious "awakening" to which the title refers) merely frames the more central plot of another, more literal, awakening. This is the tale of his daughter Lolotte, who, exasperated with poverty and hunger, rejects any claims to genteel femininity by undertaking a "man's job" to compensate for her father's inability to earn a living. Although the young woman's exploits land her in the hospital with a mild case of amnesia, she "awakens," memory intact, to discover that her father's remorse has converted him into a workaholic. However, even though her father is now a wage earner, Lolotte is retrieved from the hospital by Master Duplan, who arranges to care for her in an elevated style that her father cannot afford. In this way, Lolotte is proved to be a "lady," regardless of her economic circumstances.

Lolotte's story is critical to the ideological argument of "A Rude Awakening." At the beginning of the story, her defiance of bourgeois gender norms signals her family's lower socioeconomic standing, while, at the end, her transformation into the docile, dependent southern woman signifies her family's racial purity and, by extension, its improved social standing. Of course, neither as the dependent of a temporary worker nor, later, as the daughter of a field hand can Lolotte afford the luxuries of the bourgeois southern woman, who could rely on paid domestic labor to provide her leisure. But Bordon's improved economic status is made to coincide with Lolotte's *imitation* of ideal southern femininity when, in her condition as the submissive female patient under the paternalistic care of male doctors and benefactors, Lolotte is waited on *as if* she were a woman of economic means. Furthermore, this bourgeois lifestyle is permitted to continue at home when her prescribed prolonged period of rest is supported by the free domestic help and childcare (for her younger brothers) volunteered by her African American neighbor, Aunt Minty.

"A Rude Awakening" differs from Chopin's most celebrated story of awakening in its appeal to orthodox femininity as the remedy for prejudice based on ethnicity or class. Whereas for Edna gender works along with class to suppress a sense of selfhood, for Lolotte ideal femininity protects against class and racial discrimination. Lolotte's adherence to bourgeois gender norms — a crucial sign of the family's social respectability — opens the way to inclusion in reputable white society.

At the same time, Chopin's fiction that Lolotte could by herself, through gender conformity, achieve class mobility and white racial designation is undercut when we realize how precariously her status is buttressed by Duplan's financial support on the one hand and Aunt Minty's unpaid labor on the other. Chopin's text thus attempts to conceal what Gunning has called "the class-bound dimension of idealized whiteness" ("Kate Chopin" 73), a dimension that many post-Civil War texts worked to erase in an effort to reassert white supremacy by uniting all Caucasians against the now common enemy, the "sable" race. As Gunning asserts, Chopin's writing "engages with ever-present class, sectional, and ethnic tensions that lay below the surface of white supremacists' stereotypes of monolithic white national identities" ("Kate Chopin" 66).

Yet, even while Lolotte's identity shifts according to her class status and gender performance, her racial ambiguity ultimately allows for such shifts to take place. Consequently, Chopin situates her character squarely in the middle of the color line throughout the text, moving her closer to one end of the spectrum and then to the other. In describing Lolotte's all-important female body, Chopin employs ambiguous signifiers of racial identity such as her "brown eyes," "bare brown feet," and "eyes gr[owing] round and big, as she watched the moon creep up" (*CW* 137, 138). These attributes alarmingly point to contemporaneous portrayals of African Americans, particularly mulattoes, whose brownness indexed a tainted, tragic, halfway position between whiteness and blackness.

Although brown, however, Lolotte remains the racially unnamed and potentially white woman, especially when Chopin places her in contrast to the "fat black negress" (*CW* 139), Aunt Minty. Chopin occasionally casts Lolotte as whiter than the "negress," as in the scene in which she connects Lolotte with morality and Aunt Minty with criminality. Offering to contribute to the Bordon family's dinner a Brahma chicken that has clearly been stolen, Aunt Minty refuses to admit to any act of thievery. But Lolotte, who admonishes her neighbor not to cook the contraband fowl, considers the act immoral even if she herself should abet the crime out of dire want:

> She knew, notwithstanding her injunction, that the chicken would be cooked and eaten. Maybe she herself would partake of it when she came back, if hunger drove her too sharply.
>
> "Nax' thing I'm goen be one rogue," she muttered; and the tears gathered and fell one by one upon her cheeks. (*CW* 139)

Yet, even as Lolotte's moral sense connects her with a higher (read: whiter) social class, Chopin's fiction turns again by raising the issue of who more closely adheres to cultural norms, specifically as they apply to gender. When Lolotte realizes her father intends to neglect his newest duty, driving Duplan's mules, she takes her father's place on the wagon. This time the brown Lolotte resolves to defy cultural mores, whereas the black Aunt Minty warns against transgressing them:

> "Git down f'om dah, child! Is you plumb crazy?" she exclaimed.
>
> "No, I ain't crazy; I'm hungry, Aunt Minty. We all hungry. Somebody got fur work in dis fam'ly."
>
> "Dat ain't no work fur a gal w'at ain't bar' seventeen year ole; drivin' Marse Duplan's mules! W'at I gwine tell you' pa?" (*CW* 139)

Lolotte's disregard for gender etiquette moves her farther away from the ideal of southern womanhood and thus from the whiteness unequivocally associated with that ideal.

"Git down f'om dah, child!"

Illustration for "A Rude Awakening" printed in the *Youth's Companion*,
New England edition, *The American Periodical Series on Microfilm*, 2 February
1893, page 54. Image published with permission of ProQuest Information and
Learning Company. Further reproduction is prohibited without permission.

By exploiting Lolotte's racial ambiguity throughout the text, Chopin's argument in favor of Cajun whiteness packs a bigger punch at the story's end when, in a revelatory moment, readers learn that Lolotte is not even so much as part black; rather, she is entirely white. Chopin employs color as a sign of both race and social class distinction in the final scene, when, following her hospital stay, Lolotte is admitted to the Duplans' drawing room. As Lolotte awaits reunion with her family and friends, the suspense builds, not just because her loved ones will learn that she is alive (a secret in which the reader shares), but also because everyone, characters and reader alike, will discover that Lolotte has been transformed into the epitome of exalted white southern femininity:

> She was almost as white as the gown she wore. Her neatly shod feet rested upon a cushion, and her black hair, that had been closely cut, was beginning to make little rings about her temples. (*CW* 143)

> "An' dah you is!" almost shouted aunt Minty, whose black face gleamed in the doorway; "dah you is, settin' down, lookin' jis' like w'ite folks!"
> "Ain't I always was w'ite folks, Aunt Mint?" smiled Lolotte, feebly.
> "G'long, chile. You knows me. I don' mean no harm." (*CW* 144)

When the white tableau of Lolotte sitting in the Duplans' drawing room is juxtaposed against this later exchange between Lolotte and Aunt Minty, it is easy to see how Chopin's representations of colored bodies in these passages act as semantic markers that "speak" each character's class and race. In the first passage, Lolotte remains ambiguous — potentially black — because, although her literally white-robed body connects her with a higher social class, that connection is simultaneously undercut by Chopin's description of the black hair curling around her face. Chopin prolongs the suspense to the very last second, when she constructs Aunt Minty's observations as a simile rather than a declarative statement; Aunt Minty notes not that Lolotte *is* white but that she looks "jis' *like* w'ite folks." Only in Lolotte's response does Chopin allow the text to disclose the deepest secret of her story: that the poor, dark, transgressive young woman, whose speech patterns differ from those of hegemonic Anglo-Saxon culture, has acculturated and thus become white.[27]

In employing the language of racial difference to describe the change that she sees in Lolotte, Aunt Minty makes reference to class stratification, which produces ethnic categories within racial fields. Paradoxically, Lolotte's confusion on this issue actually clarifies the point. When Aunt Minty observes that, seated in the elegant drawing room and clothed in finery, Lolotte looks "jis' like w'ite folks," Lolotte questions, "Ain't I always was w'ite folks, Aunt Mint?" Lolotte uses the color-coded term "white" purely as a signifier of race, while Aunt Minty employs it more appropriately to designate Lolotte's gender conformity and newly up-lifted social class. Recognizing the potential racial slur she has just leveled against her racial superior (although, until now, her economic equal), Aunt Minty is quick to apologize for any misunderstanding: "G'long, chile. You knows me. I don' mean no harm."

These words end Lolotte's tale. The remaining few lines revert to the story's frame. With Sylveste secure in the knowledge of his daughter's good health, he is prepared to benefit from the moral issued by his benefactor:

> "And now, Sylveste," said Mr. Duplan, as he rose and started to walk the floor, with hands in his pockets, "listen to me. It will be a long time before Lolotte is strong again. Aunt Minty is going to look after things for you till the child is fully recovered. But what I want to say is this: I shall trust these children into your hands once more, and I want you never to forget again that you are their father — do you hear? — *that you are a man!*"
>
> Old Sylveste stood with his hand in Lolotte's, who rubbed it lovingly against her cheek.
>
> "By gracious! M'sieur Duplan," he answered, "w'en God want to he'p me, I'm goen try my bes'!" (*CW* 144; emphasis added)

Sylveste Bordon's journey toward legitimate white manhood is achieved through his embrace of steady, wage-producing work, and his achievement is signaled by his daughter's bourgeois appearance and actions as she comforts him with a typically feminine, silent gesture of support. The tale closes with Sylveste attributing his good fortune to God, a discursive move that conflates divine intervention with the guidance of the Creole planter Joe Duplan. Thus, Duplan's elevated paternal status and Sylveste's newly found devotion to those more powerful than he (God and the godlike Duplan) reassure readers that, with Cajun labor's subordination to Creole capital, all is right in the world. *Companion* readers thus get a lesson in how white Anglo-Saxon Protestant values — industry, labor, and noblesse oblige — apply differently to Cajun and Creole men: They break Cajuns in to disciplined work, demonstrating for (an assumed white male managerial class of) readers the success of self-regulating Christian values in controlling labor, and they require privileged white, planter/capital-class Creoles to kindly take care of their own.

3

For the Love of Children

Motherhood Lore, Childhood Lore, and the Matter of Prejudice in Five Companion Tales

The middle decades of the nineteenth century in America attached heretofore unprecedented importance to "mothering" — woman's work of caring for and nurturing children — and its relevance to the period's definitions of ideal feminity. Ann Douglas has written of the period's emphasis on maternity, claiming that mid-nineteenth-century "American culture seemed bent on establishing a perpetual Mother's Day"; and Stephanie Smith's conclusion that in the period, "'mother,' for all intents and purposes, meant 'woman,'" corroborates the notion that a mid-nineteenth-century female did not meet definitions of True Womanhood unless she was also "motherly." [1]

Mary Ryan has termed that midcentury period "The Empire of the Mother," a phrase Ryan took from the title of an 1870s book authored by Henry C. Wright.[2] Wright's text simply iterated the period's already well-established discourse on maternity, which claimed that mothers could affect nations through the values they instilled in their children. So accepted was this concept of mothers' empire that Catharine Beecher could expect to be taken seriously in 1845 when she wrote with dramatic flair, "American women! Will you save your country?" in her attempt to marshal women to the collective task of righting the immoral world outside the home by ministering to their husbands and children (qtd. in Ryan 40). Imbued with such far-reaching powers, domestic femininity, coupled with its ideological mandate for maternal nurture, constituted every woman's patriotic duty.

However, woman's *duty* to mother increasingly became represented as woman's *nature* to mother, especially since, as Ryan has noted, the ideological power of imperial motherhood began to decline around the same time that a romantic discourse on childhood began to emerge.[3] Between roughly 1850 and 1900, the Romantic child was a stable and recognizable type not only in popular and professional discourses but also in children's fiction.[4] The emergence of the Romantic child as a discursive construct in English and American discourses is typically credited to the influence of Jean-Jacques Rousseau's *Emile*, which was first published in France in 1762.[5] Whereas eighteenth-century Puritan and Calvinist doctrine asserted that people were born as essentially depraved creatures, Rousseau's *Emile* claimed that they were born naturally innocent and that the period from birth to age twelve constituted an "age of nature" in which children, if protected from environmental corruption, maintained their fundamental purity.[6]

Anne Scott MacLeod locates Rousseau's earliest influence in juvenile fiction in the late eighteenth-century stories of Maria Edgeworth (MacLeod, *American Childhood* 143–56). Although Edgeworth was British, her children's stories were widely read and imitated in the United States. MacLeod contends that Edgeworth's fiction reflects a combination of both old and new thought, the old being eighteenth-century rationalism and the new, the kernels of nineteenth-century Romanticism. MacLeod articulates Edgeworth's trademark as being the representation of child characters who, though imperfect creatures, are nonetheless reasonable and have a *natural capacity* for goodness. These child models learn by their mistakes, along with benevolent admonitions by adults who make clear to them the error of their ways. Although MacLeod admits these child characters are idealized — they always learn their lesson the first time around — she distinguishes them from what she calls the "sentimental," or Romantic, child characters of midcentury, who were a mainstay of both British and American juvenile fiction until the turn of the century. This sentimentalized child, so perfectly angelic that he or she has lessons to teach adults, is most commonly referred to as the Rousseauesque, or Romantic, child.[7]

Although Ryan has noted that the Romantic child, a literary type who was "somehow outside of, and superior to, [her] mother's tutelage" (*Empire* 145), worked to undermine both the value of maternal nurture at home and the power of domestic femininity at large, no one has considered what impact these two constructs' simultaneous emergence and disappearance had on discourses of femininity and maternity in the last decades of the century. In an age when birth control methods were becoming more widely understood by and available to white bourgeois women; when the women's suffrage movement increased discussions of women's rights and freedoms; and when a construct called the "New Woman" had just begun circulating in the 1890s, touting women's abilities to be "single, highly educated, [and] economically autonomous" (Smith-Rosenberg 245), the Romantic child served to convince women that their place continued to be in the home, married, domestically inclined, and economically dependent. Thus, the construct of the Romantic child worked to naturalize woman's maternal "instincts," such that True Women were signified by their inability to resist the (sentimentalized) pleasures of loving a child. Though reproductivity may not have been late-nineteenth-century woman's destiny (to the same degree as it was for midcentury woman), the inescapable love of children was.

Five of Chopin's *Youth's Companion* stories, "A Matter of Prejudice," "Loka," "Beyond the Bayou," "Mamouche," and "Polydore" draw upon romanticized discourses of childhood in order to further sentimentalize woman's maternal "instincts" and thereby reify motherhood. Because these five texts are unlike Chopin's more trenchant feminist critiques in that they either do the work of naturalizing or subscribe to already-naturalized concepts of woman's maternal role, they serve as examples of how Chopin's feminism is moderated by her classist, regionalist, and racial interests. As such, these texts illustrate both how and why it is distorting merely to read Chopin's work through the one-dimensional lens of gender. Because Chopin's texts are concerned with *both* gender bias against white middle-class women *and* racial, ethnic, and class biases against Louisiana Creoles and Cajuns, we can explain Chopin's alternately subversive and orthodox deployments of femininity by pinpointing whose political interests she is attempting to serve.

"A MATTER OF PREJUDICE"

In "A Matter of Prejudice," Chopin romanticizes both childhood and motherhood to obtain for a French Creole woman an "interior" of feminine universality that prevails over her "exterior" of ethnic particularity. Through her character's inability to escape the Romantic child's transformational charms, Chopin naturalizes her Creole character's maternal feelings. Thus, for her love of children, Chopin's ethnic Creole female becomes culturally intelligible as a universal True Woman, which, in essence, elides her external ethnic differences.[8]

The story centers around Madame Carambeau, a widowed Creole matron in the French Quarter of New Orleans who overcomes her prejudice against Americans when circumstances compel her to take a sick American child into her home and nurse her back to health. Caring for the small girl melts Madame Carambeau's hardened heart, and the little one's departure makes the Creole widow lonely enough to reconcile with her estranged son and his American wife, of whose "mixed" marriage she vehemently disapproved.

Upon entering her son's home in the American Quarter for the first time on Christmas Day, Madame Carambeau learns that her formerly sick charge is her very own half-Creole, half-American grandchild, and the only remaining obstacle facing their relationship is that the two cannot communicate because they speak different languages. Madame Carambeau's daughter-in-law apologizes profusely for this temporary obstacle separating granddaughter and grandmother:

> "I am so sorry, ma mère," she said, "that our little one does not speak French. It is not my fault, I assure you," and she flushed and hesitated a little. "It — it was Henri who would not permit it."
>
> "That is nothing," replied madame, amiably, drawing the child close to her. "Her grandmother will teach her French; and she will teach her grandmother English. You see, I have no prejudices. I am not like my son. Henri was always a stubborn boy. Heaven only knows how he came by such a character!" (*CW* 288)

This ending to the story is both humorous and instructive, for the reader knows Henri "came by such a character" through his mother. Early on in the story, Chopin describes "old Madame Carambeau" as "a woman of many prejudices — so many, in fact, that it would be difficult to name them all. She detested dogs, cats, organ-grinders, white servants and children's noises. She despised Americans, Germans and all people of a different faith from her own. Anything not French had, in her opinion, little right to existence" (*CW* 282).

can culture. This departure from gender norms, along with Madame Carambeau's "foreign" ways, do not empower her but rather make her susceptible to the same kinds of prejudice that she harbors against others.

Madame Carambeau deviates from gender norms in another way as well, and that is in her expert skill as a nurse. Although ministering to the sick was traditional woman's work, particularly in the South, where plantation homes were distant from urban medical facilities and doctors,[9] Chopin describes Madame Carambeau more as an expert medical practitioner than as a naturally endowed care-giver: "Though she was a creature of prejudice, she was nevertheless a skilled and accomplished nurse, and a connoisseur in all matters pertaining to health. She prided herself upon this talent, and never lost an opportunity of exercising it. She would have treated an organ-grinder with tender consideration if one had presented himself in the character of an invalid" (CW 283). Rather than attribute her nursing ability to the nurturing capacity inherent in all women, Chopin treats it as something Madame has painstakingly acquired through experience.

It is, however, in this traditional role as care-giver that Madame Carambeau undergoes the "change of heart" that encourages her to rethink the root cause of one of her prejudices:

> Madame, in all her varied experience with the sick, had never before nursed so objectionable a character as an American child. But the trouble was that after the little one went away, she could think of nothing really objectionable against her except the accident of her birth, which was, after all, her misfortune; and her ignorance of the French language, which was not her fault. (CW 285)

Thus, the (Romantic) baby's transformational charms bring out Madame Carambeau's natural maternal instincts.

Chopin paints the effect the child has on Madame as a seduction: "But the touch of the caressing baby arms; the pressure of the soft little body in the night; the tones of the voice, and the feeling of the hot lips when the child kissed her, believing herself to be with her mother, were impressions that had sunk through the crust of madame's prejudice and reached her heart" (CW 285). Chopin's language in the preceding passage constructs Madame Carambeau's character as having both an inside and an outside, an exterior "crust" of prejudice and an interior "heart" of sentimental femininity. For the love of a child, indeed her own grandchild, Madame Carambeau's core of essential motherliness is "touched," enabling her to overcome her prejudices against Americans. But, more important, the text works to soften "American" readers' prejudices against Madame Carambeau, since this proud, stubborn, externally different Creole Other's essential feminine likeness is recuperated by her conformity to orthodox notions of maternal womanhood. It is a strategy Chopin deploys in another story about a Native American woman, but for different effect.

"LOKA"

"Loka" is Chopin's short story about a teenage, half-Choctaw Indian girl who nearly leaves the Cajun family that keeps her but stays for her love of the family's baby, Bibine. As in "A Matter of Prejudice," Chopin relies upon romanticized discourses of childhood to naturalize Loka's innate love of children. But here is where the analogy stops, for unlike Madame Carambeau, Loka is not completely white. Though Loka's partial whiteness allows for an idealization of her maternal instincts, her half-Native American ancestry renders her fundamentally different from other white women in the text, of whom Chopin is admittedly critical, but for whom there are defined and even privileged positions in society.

Loka's "half-breed" status, however, disallows her a similarly defined social place. In its subscription to a signifying system that codes whiteness as human and redness as savage, Chopin's text searches for a solution to the problem of what to do with a part-human, part-animal creature such as Loka. Thus, the narrative treats Loka less as a sympathetic subject than as an object through which to teach white southerners a kinder, gentler management style for governing people of color.

To read Loka as object rather than subject is not a new approach. Bonner has already observed that Chopin uses Loka as a "device" to criticize existing forms of philanthropy in her day.[10] When Loka "appeared one day at the side door of Frobissaint's 'oyster saloon' in Natchitoches, asking for food, Frobissaint, a practical philanthropist, engaged her on the spot as a tumbler-washer " (*CW* 212). Frobissaint's form of "practical philanthropy," which Chopin satirizes, is his unwillingness to give something for nothing or, put another way, his willingness to give as long as what he gets in return is an even trade. When Frobissaint discovers that Loka is "not successful" as a tumbler washer because she "br[eaks] too many tumblers" (CW 212), he simply "charge[s] her with the broken glasses" (CW 212), a move that illustrates just how completely unconcerned he is with the economic condition in which he found Loka, with "hardly a rag to her back" (CW 212). His morality is an eye-for-an-eye economics, which will keep Loka in perpetual poverty.

So Chopin's narrative does not so much sympathize with Loka as it does criticize white folks' handling of her. Chopin's authorial treatment of Loka lacks a fundamental identification with her precisely on the basis of her difference, which Chopin exploits to render Loka basically inferior to and consequently inassimilable into the white community as an equal. Thus, Chopin racializes Loka by ascribing to her Native American heritage — her red-skinned race — natural and inevitable qualities that Loka can neither change nor modify. Loka's clumsiness as a tumbler washer is a stereotyped outgrowth of her Choctaw background, as is her violence, which surfaces in the form of her breaking tumblers "over the heads" of Frobissaint's customers. Even Loka's physical attributes are described as stereotyped "red" racial characteristics: "Loka was not beautiful, as she stood in her red calico rags before the scrutinizing band. Her coarse, black, unkempt hair framed a broad, swarthy face without a redeeming feature, except eyes that were not bad; slow in their movements, but frank eyes enough. She was big-boned and clumsy (CW 212)." Just as Loka's bigness, clumsiness, and violence are directly connected to her savage race, so are her ugliness, mental thickness, and lack of motivation.

The "scrutinizing band" before which Loka appears is the Band of United Endeavor, an unsympathetic group of white women married to community leaders such as the local minister, judge, doctor, and planter and who have nothing better to do with their time than meddle in other people's affairs. Loka is brought to the band's attention by Frobissaint, who drags her there when she doesn't turn out to be a grateful and compliant dishwasher: "[H]e seized her by the wrist and dragged her before the Band of United Endeavor, then in session around the corner. This was considerate on Frobissaint's part, for he could have dragged her just as well to the police station" (CW 212). Chopin's sarcasm in defending

Frobissaint's "considerateness" by taking Loka before the Band of United Endeavor instead of the police is clearly a critique of the available venues for "placing" Loka. Just as Loka's half-whiteness made her leave Bayou Choctaw because she did not want to "cheat, to beg and lie" (*CW* 215), her half-Choctaw "nature" leaves her with no place to go in the white community. However, even though Chopin's text registers the fact that there is no cultural space for Loka to inhabit, it also reinscribes Loka's "no-place" status by racializing her. All but one member of "the band" reject the idea of sending Loka to a reformatory, precisely because Loka's Native American savagery cannot be reformed.

Consequently, Chopin writes that Loka is "paroled" to the Padues, a word that indicates her dual alien and captive (racial) status. The band's intent for this "respectable family of 'Cadians . . . [to] give the girl a home, with benefit to all concerned" (*CW* 212), further illustrates how Loka's white status is forever qualified by her red race, so that Loka's parole is more like indentured servitude without the promise of release. Loka is meant to work night and day around the Padue home, a containment Chopin metaphorizes through the enclosure of Loka's big, clumsy feet in the customary "brogans," ankle-high work shoes that signify her imprisonment: "Loka was afraid of treading upon the little Padues when she first got amongst them, — there were so many of them, — and her feet were like leaden weights, encased in the strong brogans with which the band had equipped her" (*CW* 213).

Loka's work-detail director is Tontine, the Cajun woman who is mistress of the household and whom Chopin describes as a colonizer who wishes Loka to acculturate fully to her French Cajun ways. "'How come you don't talk French, you?'" she asks Loka accusingly in the most oppressive kind of colonialist impulse, while she accordingly orders Loka to "fo'git yo' Choctaw," a pronouncement that expresses how completely Tontine wants Loka to give up her native culture and assume Tontine's own.

Furthermore, Tontine believes Loka's native savagery has "got to be work out of her" (*CW* 213), a belief that turns Tontine, already "a good deal more fussy . . . than her easy-going husband and children thought necessary or agreeable" (*CW* 213), into a virtual slave driver. However, the lesson that Tontine must learn in governing Loka is what the text articulates over and over again: that Loka's racial characteristics will not change. Chopin's narrative is explicit in its assertion that Loka is not entirely free from blame and that Tontine is somewhat justified in her exasperation:

> The girl was indeed so deliberate about her tasks that she had to be urged constantly to accomplish the amount of labor that Tontine required of her. Moreover, she carried to her work a stolid indifference that was exasperating. Whether at the wash-tub, scrubbing the floors, weeding the garden, or learning her lessons and catechism with the children on Sundays, it was the same. (*CW* 213)

The only time Loka's motivation changes is when she is with the Padues' baby, Bibine. Loka's sentimental feelings for the infant bespeak the white half of her heritage, connecting her, as they do, with romanticized constructions of maternal (white) womanhood:

> It was only when intrusted [*sic*] with the care of little Bibine, the baby, that Loka crept somewhat out of her apathy. She grew very fond of him. No wonder; such a baby as he was! So good, so fat, and complaisant! He had such a way of clasping Loka's broad face between his pudgy fists and savagely biting her chin with his hard, toothless gums! Such a way of bouncing in her arms as if he were mounted upon springs! At his antics the girl would laugh a wholesome, ringing laugh that was good to hear. (*CW* 213–14)

Loka's whiteness, signified by her love of Bibine, is what imparts wholesomeness to her otherwise tainted character. These two halves of Loka struggle for dominance when she is left alone with Bibine after the rest of the Padues go to town on a shopping trip. Away from the remonstrances of Madame Padue, Loka is free to daydream about her previous life of freedom on Bayou Choctaw: "How good it felt to walk with moccasined feet over the springy turf, under the trees! What fun to trap the squirrels, to skin the otter; to take those swift flights on the pony that Choctaw Joe had stolen from the Texans!" (*CW* 215). Loka thinks briefly that for such freedom, it is worth enduring "old Marot, the squaw who drank whiskey and plaited baskets and beat her. . . . She could not feel just then that the sin and pain of that life were anything beside the joy of its freedom" (*CW* 215).

In a scene symbolizing the restrictions placed on her while in the Padues' care, Loka "unlaced the brogans that were chafing her feet, removed them and her stockings, and threw the things away from her" (*CW* 215). Pining for her past, Loka prepares to escape. "But there was a sound that stopped her. It was little Bibine, cooing, sputtering, battling hands and feet with the mosquito net that he had dragged over his face. The girl uttered a sob as she reached down for the baby she had grown to love so, and clasped him in her arms. She could not go and leave Bibine behind" (*CW* 215–16).

Although Loka settles for a walk with the baby in the woods, neither readers nor the Padues, when they return to find Loka and Bibine absent, know where she has taken him. Thus, Madame Padue fears the worst. The family organizes a search party, which after only a short while, retrieves Loka and her little charge. Madame Padue, unmoved by Loka's explanation that she and Bibine were merely walking, threatens to send Loka away. Loka's response is highly emotional:

> "Don' sen' me 'way frum Bibine," entreated the girl, with a note in her voice like lament.
>
> "Today," she went on, in her dragging manner, "I want to run 'way bad, an' take to de wood; an' go yonda back to Bayou Choctaw to steal an' lie agin. It's on'y Bibine w'at hole me back. I could n'lef' 'im. I could n' do dat. An' we jis' go take lit' 'broad in de wood, das all, him an' me. Don' sen' me 'way like dat!" (*CW* 217)

Perhaps, as her name suggests, what is "crazy" about Loka is that she chooses to stay in a physical place that manifests her cultural place as indentured servitude.[11] But the power of idealized maternal womanhood wins out in the struggle between (white) goodness and (red) savagery inside Loka. Though the girl's decision to stay wins her compassion from the family's patriarch, it is also Baptiste who reminds us that it is only in maternal femininity that Loka's whiteness comes through. Counseling his wife that Loka "ent like you an' me, po' thing; she's one Injun, her" (*CW* 218), Baptiste renders Loka not only culturally but essentially different from other white Cajuns. He entreats Tontine to heed the following

Loka Longs for Her Old Life

Illustration for "Loka" printed in the *Youth's Companion*, New England edition, *The American Periodical Series on Microfilm*, 22 December 1892, page 670. Image published with permission of ProQuest Information and Learning Company. Further reproduction is prohibited without permission.

message: "You been grind that girl too much. She ent a bad girl — I been watch her close, 'count of the chil'ren; she ent bad. All she want, it's li'le mo' rope. You can't drive a ox with the same gearin' you drive a mule. You got to learn that, Tontine" (*CW* 218).

Not stubborn like a mule, but big, dumb, and slow like an ox, Loka — as Baptiste's comments reinscribe her — is a benign but dense creature who requires a special kind of management. Because of Loka's essential difference, Baptiste argues, she can be kept, managed, and cared for effectively only if he and his wife subscribe to the New Southern Paternalism's codes of conduct. Although Tontine, a strong-willed woman, has governed Loka up to this point in the text, Baptiste now becomes "determined to profit by his wife's lachrymose and wilted condition to assert his authority" (*CW* 217) and positions himself as "masta in this house" (*CW* 217). With Baptiste now firmly established as head of the household, Tontine, his wife, silently and passively listening, and Loka, the racial Other in voluntary servitude, Chopin realigns the heretofore out-of-place cultural hierarchy in the Padue home. Rather than subvert existing social power relations, Chopin imagines an ending wherein all is right with the world because the Christian status quo of familial (and racial) structures is kept in place.

"BEYOND THE BAYOU"

"Beyond the Bayou" is yet another tale that grapples with the issue of the cultural and physical place in society of a woman of color. Its central character is Jacqueline, a former slave described after the war as a "large, gaunt black woman, past thirty-five" (*CW* 175), who has not since her youth ventured beyond the bayou that encircles her cabin. Chopin's description of Jacqueline's fear of external spaces conforms with current definitions of "agoraphobia," an anxiety Jacqueline manifested as a child when her young, white plantation master, P'tit Maître, entered her cabin "black with powder and crimson with blood" (*CW* 175) after being shot in a local Civil War skirmish. The sight frightened the youthful Jacqueline "literally 'out of her senses'" (*CW* 175), causing her to inherit the nickname "La Folle" to signify the phobia that has kept her on her own side of the bayou ever since.

Although Ewell and Toth each have claimed that "Beyond the Bayou" is about the residual traumas of war,[12] suggesting, as they do, that Jacqueline's agoraphobia stems from the irrational belief that stepping off one's property will cause one to get shot, it is also about the boundaries of place restricting the freedom of women of color in the late nineteenth-century South. Because P'tit Maître was fighting for the right to govern his property as he saw fit when he was injured, the moral rumbling beneath the surface of the tale for Jacqueline, an ex-slave, is that it is dangerous to exercise one's right to control one's destiny under the shadow of a more powerful social group. Although in the world of the text the masters and mistresses of Bellissime are accepting of Jacqueline's newfound independence at the story's end, as a black woman in the Victorian South, Jacqueline is not at all crazy in her assumption that she is safer in a segregated realm far removed from the domain of privilege "beyond the bayou" where the white characters live.

Thus, the physical space Jacqueline occupies beyond even the Negro quarters at Bellissime can be read as a metaphor for her marginalized cultural place within the social hierarchy. Though Chopin's text registers this inequality of racialized physical and cultural "places," the story recasts the social reality of ubiquitous black oppression as Jacqueline's personal phobia, an "irrational" fear that is hers alone to overcome and for which compassionate white folk, such as those at Bellissime, are certainly not to blame.

Consequently, "Beyond the Bayou" resolves Jacqueline's oppression — coded here as obsession — in ways that are acceptable and nonthreatening to a white readership. For the love of a white child, Jacqueline is allowed to overstep the segregated boundaries of her physical and cultural place. In a scene many years later that parallels P'tit Maître's Civil War injury, P'tit Maître's son, a ten-year-old whom Jacqueline has nicknamed Chéri, accidentally shoots himself in the leg in woods near Jacqueline's home. The only one within earshot of the accident, Jacqueline is faced with the irreconcilable desires of either saving the boy by carrying him across the bayou to Bellissime or protecting herself. In a moment of desperation, she chooses the boy's welfare over her own and, upon crossing the bayou, safely delivers Chéri home.

Chopin's text both allows and contains Jacqueline's defiant act of exceeding the boundaries of her metaphorical place by drawing upon the familiar literary figure of the black mammy. Chopin's representation of Jacqueline references what Catherine Juanita Starke has called "fictional symbols of inferior foster mothers" in southern fiction.[13] Chopin negates Jacqueline's womanhood, writing that Jacqueline "had more physical strength than most men, and made her patch of cotton and corn and tobacco like the best of them" (*CW* 175). Jacqueline's blackness signifies that she is about as far from the ideal of delicate white womanhood as one can get. Chopin's depiction of Jacqueline's strength and size works not only to separate her from ideals of nineteenth-century womanhood but also to connect her with a species of large, dumb, plowing animals. The fact that Chopin claims Jacqueline "was sorry when [the cows were sent to pasture,] for she loved these dumb companions well" (*CW* 176); that, when Jacqueline was carrying Chéri across the bayou, "she breathed heavily, as a tired ox" (*CW* 178); and that, when Jacqueline finally reached the great stairs to the veranda of Bellissime, "she fell heavily to the ground" (*CW* 178) all demonstrate how Chopin's rhetoric draws upon aspects of nineteenth-century racial discourse that represented blackness as bestial.

However, Jacqueline's "bestiality" is nonetheless domesticated — and thus, rendered harmless — through her love of a white child, specifically, the adolescent son of P'tit Maître. Chopin writes that although P'tit Maître had

> a family of beautiful daughters about him, [he also had] a little son whom La Folle loved as if he had been her own. She called him Chéri, and so did every one else because she did.
>
> None of the girls had ever been to her what Chéri was. They had each and all loved to be with her, and to listen to her wondrous stories of things that always happened "yonda, beyon' de bayou."
>
> But none of them had stroked her black hand quite as Chéri did, nor rested their heads against her knee so confidingly, nor fallen asleep in her arms as he used to do. (*CW* 175–76)

This depiction of a black maternal figure who loves the plantation master's child as deeply as she might have loved her own functions in Chopin's

1893 story as justification for continued white dominance, just as the stock literary type of the black mammy worked in antebellum fiction to legitimize black enslavement.

Significantly, too, Jacqueline continues to love Chéri as he approaches manhood and becomes the heir apparent master of Bellissime and its black tenants. Even during "that summer," when Chéri "had become the proud possessor of a gun, and had had his black curls cut off" (*CW* 176), Jacqueline spent her time tediously making croquignoles (a kind of biscuit or pastry) of various shapes to please the boy in the mere chance he should come to visit.

Thus, surprising as it is to the residents and tenants of Bellissime, it should come as no surprise to readers that Jacqueline undertakes her mad trek across the bayou and beyond to do whatever she believes is necessary to save Chéri's life after the shooting. What is surprising is that Jacqueline's journey effectively cures her phobia and opens up a new world to the ex-slave in more ways than one. After Jacqueline has safely delivered Chéri home, she faints from exhaustion, is carried back to her cabin, and, somewhat miraculously, recovers by the next morning. This time, choosing of her own accord to make a second trip across the bayou, Jacqueline ascends the great stairs of Bellissime and confronts the plantation mistress by inquiring after Chéri. Told by Chéri's mother that the boy is sleeping and asked to return later, Jacqueline instead settles the matter upon her own terms, exclaiming, "*Non*, madame. I'm goin' wait yair tell Chéri wake up" (*CW* 180). Thus, in asserting her own will against white authority, Jacqueline not only transgresses the physical boundaries that limit her freedom; she also challenges the social codes that require her subordination to white hegemony.

Because Jacqueline leaves her domain this second time of her own will and bidding, Chopin's text suggests the ex-slave merely imagined the bayou as a segregating barrier between herself and the world of white privilege beyond. After all, upon entering this privileged white space at Bellissime, Jacqueline challenges the white authority of Chéri's mother with no discriminatory effects. Chopin thus ends her tale with a description of how Jacqueline "watched for the first time the sun rise upon the new, the beautiful world beyond the bayou," (*CW* 180) an intimation that her achievement has political as well as personal ramifications.

As in Chopin's other texts about female emancipation, Jacqueline experiences an explosion of sensory stimuli that suggests her liberation of person as well as of physical place.[14] Chopin writes that Jacqueline

> found herself upon the border of a field where the white, bursting cotton, with the dew upon it, gleamed for acres and acres like frosted silver in the early dawn . . . [that she felt] the broad stretch of velvety lawn that surrounded the house . . . beneath her tread . . . [and that she discovered] those perfumes that were assailing her senses with memories from a time far gone . . . were . . . the thousand blue violets that peeped out from green, luxuriant beds. . . . [T]hey were . . . the big waxen bells of the magnolias far above her head, and . . . the jessamine clumps around her. (*CW* 179–80)

Thus, Chopin's text suggests that, like phobic obsession, racial oppression is Jacqueline's to overcome, and overcome it she does, with valiant success and pride. However, it is important to remember the means by which Chopin renders excusable Jacqueline's defiant act of transgressing the boundaries of her cultural place: That defiance is motivated by her love for a white child. Thus, the degree to which we can read Jacqueline's personal triumph (over her mental and emotional anxiety) as a cultural liberation (from racial confinement) is limited at best since overcoming one's personal fears is not analogous to changing the minds of those who actually govern the spaces in which one lives.

Although in both "Beyond the Bayou" and "Loka" it is tempting to celebrate Chopin's understanding of the restrictions experienced by women of color in the turn-of-the-century South, we must modify our praise proportionate to Chopin's modification of "colored" female agency through her use of racial rhetoric and Romantic childhood lore. To see just how differently Chopin deploys such discourses elsewhere, we need only turn to two other *Companion* tales, whose main concerns were coloring two Cajun boys white.

"MAMOUCHE" AND "POLYDORE"

Kate Chopin's short story "Mamouche" was published in the *Youth's Companion* on 19 April 1894; "Polydore" came out almost two years later to the day, on 23 April 1896. Although "Mamouche" was only

Chopin's sixth, and "Polydore" her eighth, story to be printed in the *Companion*, by the time of their publication, Chopin was already nationally recognized as a female local color author of Louisiana stories. Her first collection of short fiction, *Bayou Folk*, had appeared just one month before in March 1894; her first novel, *At Fault*, had been out since 1890; and more than thirty of her short stories had already circulated in the nation's daily, weekly, and monthly mass media.

By 1894, then, Chopin's texts began to assume that her predominantly non-southern readership and northern periodical editors understood "Creole" to be an elite white ethnic category in Louisiana's complex racial makeup, a category that much of her earlier fiction was dedicated to constructing. Although all of Chopin's texts self-consciously articulate the Creole as a white, Louisiana ethnic category in relation to a hegemonic northern Anglo-Saxon Protestant norm, the (mythologized) white Creoles of her fiction remain the privileged, dominant social group in the mediated Louisiana world that she presents to her readers.

Departing from her earlier texts, which focused on Creole identity, "Mamouche" and "Polydore" instead work to establish the Cajun as a French American ethnic category that is distinguished from Creole ethnicity by its lower-class status but which nevertheless belongs to the white race. Chopin's fictional distinctions between Cajun and Creole ethnicities come at the tail end of a discursive campaign begun in the 1870s by privileged white Creole sympathizers who deployed the myth that "Creole" referred exclusively to "a native Louisianian of pure white blood descended from those French and Spanish pioneers who came directly from Europe to colonize the New World" (Tregle 132). Thus, her tales reference a historical movement that had "rigorously excluded" Cajuns (by virtue of socioeconomic class difference) from the Creole community because Cajuns "arrived in the colony not straight from the Continent but by way of Canada" (Tregle 132).

By articulating the Cajuns as yet another white ethnic category, Chopin's texts attempt to make amends for Cajuns' exclusion from the protections of whiteness, exclusions encouraged by a more socially advantaged sector who made claims to Creole identity. However, her stories participate in the preservation of Creole privilege by demarcating these French American ethnicities along class lines. Through the metaphor of adoption, Chopin figures Creoles as benefactors and Cajuns as orphans whose convenient complementariness provides the rationale for their familial integration. Her fictions appropriate Creole whiteness for Cajuns presumably because, in order to become family members, Cajuns and Creoles must be fundamentally of the same racial ilk. However, although Creoles' adoption of Cajuns confirms the latter's biological whiteness, Chopin's texts mandate that Cajuns also adopt white American values and behaviors in order to signify themselves as a white-acculturated ethnic group.

"Mamouche" and "Polydore," then, were compatible with the *Youth's Companion*'s politics in their themes of class unification and assimilation. Both stories' nod to northern white, Anglo-Saxon Protestant standards of behavior, along with their reinscription of "ethnic division among whites themselves" (Gunning, *Race* 125), decidedly mark them as regionalist fiction. Chopin's fictions of privileged white Creoles taking in wayward and needy Cajuns accommodated northern periodical editors' endorsement of noblesse oblige as the means by which to resolve social conflict within a heterogeneous white population. The underclass recruit in question — in this case, the Cajun — is safely admitted to the white mainstream by a paternalistic escort — in this case, the Creole — whose presence ensures that the recruit is a creditable inductee.

The Creole's endorsement of the Cajun outsider in these texts affirms not only that the Cajun is biologically white but also that the Creole benefactor will commit to teaching him how to behave as such. In this way, the metaphor of adoption is applicable to both sides. Even though it is Creoles' responsibility to love their French Canadian "cousins" enough to accept them into the nuclear family unit and thereby usher them into reputable white society, it is also Cajuns' job to adopt privileged white American culture by agreeing to engage in the work of self-management and internal reform.

Of all of Chopin's stories published in the *Companion*, "Mamouche" and "Polydore," along with "A Matter of Prejudice," most closely resemble other contemporaneous texts that the academy has since come to categorize as children's literature. These two stories' prescriptive messages are presented in didactic formats that act as moral exempla of how both elite (Creole) and non-elite (Cajun) white Americans should behave. By imagining the dependent Cajun as a child and the beneficent Creole as a parent, Chopin is able to draw upon nineteenth-century romantic discourses of childhood in order to depict her Cajun child characters as essentially innocent creatures in need of guidance, as opposed to predetermined depraved creatures in need of salvation.[15]

Furthermore, by choosing to depict Cajuns as children in these stories, Chopin recasts an existing black racial discourse surrounding Cajun "nature" as slothful and deviant into a simple childish immaturity that her French Canadian characters have the capacity to outgrow.[16] This important rhetorical sleight of hand works significantly to distinguish Chopin's Cajun from her African American characters. For both "Mamouche" and "Polydore" begin by replicating the tendency in Chopin's day to racialize lower-class Cajuns by imposing on them the same pejorative stereotypes of indolence and untrustworthiness that were commonly applied to racialized Others. But by suggesting the Cajuns' character deficits are a result of immature age and not biological makeup, Chopin's Cajun characters are provided with the all-important genetic provisions necessary for growth and change.

To solidify her point, Chopin's message of how the immature but naturally good white Cajun child will evolve into the responsible and acculturated good white adult is told through recognizable nineteenth-century formulae of children's fiction. Like "A Matter of Prejudice," "Polydore" operates in what Kelly has called the typical "change of heart" format, in which the main character recognizes her or his wrongs and conforms to a more socially acceptable way of life. When Polydore realizes that his thoughtlessness has caused Mamzelle Adélaïde's illness, he quite literally confesses his sins and chooses to reform of his own accord. Mamouche's conversion, on the other hand, is occasioned by his getting caught. By being forced to face his benefactor, Doctor John-Luis, whose upstanding lifestyle is placed before him as a model to emulate, Mamouche feels shame and humiliation. Thus, the story "Mamouche" conforms more to the formula of the "gentry mission" tale, one in which "the civilizing possibilities of the code of the gentleman are acted out. . . . [At the core] of the gentry mission is a figure who embodies the moral values of gentility and whose moral force brings about a change in the values of others" (Kelly, *Mother* 47–48).

Kelly further notes that conflict in the gentry mission and change-of-heart formulae is often resolved by the wayward character's return to a belief in God. Religion, then, becomes the regulatory agent that keeps the character in question in obeisance and deference to a higher authority. Thus, these stories' morals of the transformational powers of religion parallel *Companion* editor Daniel Sharp Ford's belief in the power of missionary efforts to civilize what he perceived as an unruly, nonconformist underclass.

Because the two child characters in these tales are boys, Chopin's texts further replicate what Leslie Fiedler has popularized as the type of the "Good Bad Boy," whose fictional antecedents can be found in Thomas Bailey Aldrich's *The Story of a Bad Boy* (1868) and, of course, Mark Twain's *The Adventures of Tom Sawyer* (1876).[17] Fiedler writes: "The Good Bad Boy is, of course, America's vision of itself, crude and unruly in his beginnings, but endowed by his creator with an instinctive sense of what is right. Sexually as pure as any milky maiden, he is a roughneck all the same, at once potent and submissive, made to be reformed by the right woman" (268).

The fact that, for Mamouche, this "right woman" is the Virgin Mother, Mary, and, for Polydore, it is his unimpeachably good, white adoptive mother, Mamzelle Adélaïde, indicates these boy characters' difference from Chopin's northern Anglo-Saxon Protestant readership, which neither came into contact with Creole culture nor reified the Virgin Mother to the same degree as Catholic worshippers. But by deploying holy white womanhood as a construct that elides ethnic and class differences, biology becomes destiny for Mamouche directly through Stéphanie, his good and pure Cajun grandmother, and indirectly for Polydore through the majestic, nunlike Adélaïde, whose motherly love for him recuperates in full his whiteness and entitlement to social mobility.

"Mamouche," Chopin's story about the mischievous Cajun boy by the same name, begins when Mamouche is found on the doorstep of the elderly Creole bachelor, Doctor John-Luis. Chopin wrote of Mamouche one year before in "The Lilies," although because the story appeared in *Wide Awake*, which had a circulation of only 25,000, it is impossible to know how many of her readers may have been familiar with him.[18] What is clear is that the Mamouche whom we meet in the *Companion* story is the same scamp of its predecessor, "The Lilies." The major difference regarding the character in each of the two tales is that, whereas Mamouche's innocuous pranks in the first story actually bring about some good for others, his actions in the *Companion* sequel are harmful enough to necessitate his reform.

Chopin begins her story by laying bare two of her main characters' racial, ethnic, and class identities. Marshall is introduced as the "old negro" servant to his master/employer, "Old Doctor John-Luis" (*CW* 268). Although the Doctor is not named as a Creole, he is signaled as such by his European name, his profession as a physician, his comfortable standard of living, his property holdings, and his coloration as an obviously white man with formerly red hair that was "not now more than half-bleached" (*CW* 268).

Mamouche's identity, on the other hand, is rather more tenuous, for it is he — not the author, Chopin — who declares himself white. In an exchange that raises the question of whether Mamouche is simply "passing" for the superior race, the black servant Marshall begins:

> "Is you wi'te o' is you black?" he asked. "Dat w'at I wants ter know 'fo' I kiar' victuals to you in de settin'-room."
>
> "I'm w'ite, me," the boy responded, promptly.
>
> "I ain't disputin'; go ahead. All right fer dem w'at wants ter take yo' wud fer it." Doctor John-Luis coughed behind his hand and said nothing. (*CW* 268–69)

In this brief moment of uncertainty regarding Mamouche's racial identity, Chopin begins to construct the Cajun as a distinct ethnic category by playing Mamouche off of the two racially identified characters in the text, the black Marshall and the white Doctor John-Luis. Mamouche's differences from both the Doctor and the servant are marked most emphatically by language. Ironically, Chopin's standard dialectical marker for Cajun identity — the substitution of a personal pronoun for an intensive pronoun at the end of a sentence — is what makes Mamouche temporarily difficult to locate in the social order. Even though Mamouche does not speak the grammatical, standard (white) English of Doctor John-Luis, neither does he speak the black-English dialect of Marshall. Chopin's text thus positions Mamouche in a "not" space that makes him neither this nor that and, in so doing, constructs him as a floating signifier of identity whose racial referent is yet to be located.

Significantly, it is Marshall, the one who has the most to lose by performing his social role incorrectly, who first attempts to position Mamouche within the social hierarchy. Marshall's interrogation of Mamouche references the multiracial social reality of Louisiana and the function that the institution of racial difference played in prescribing proper behavior and attitudes between people. Ultimately, the question of Mamouche's identity must be deflected off of blackness, so that before Mamouche can be determined white, he must first be designated not (even partially) black.

Such a strategy explains why Chopin references black racial representations in her earliest depictions of Mamouche, such as when he appears at Doctor John-Luis's door penniless, messy, and in need of food, shelter, and warmth. Though Mamouche declares himself biologically white, Chopin represents him as culturally black in his absolute dependency on another for his basic needs. Even Doctor John-Luis's early conclusion that Mamouche "must be a tramp" because he had no specified purpose in going to the twenty-four-mile ferry aligns the boy with the unemployed and aimless, a contemporaneous stereotypical position attributed to African Americans.

But in keeping with his own personal story of identity, Mamouche tells Doctor John-Luis that "No; I don' b'lieve I'm a tramp, me" (*CW* 269), so that the good doctor finally settles the question of Mamouche's identity on the issue of his name and ancestry. Mamouche's ability to name his forefathers two generations back definitively separates him from African Americans, many of whom, only thirty years after the abolition of slavery, had not yet had the right to maintain an unbroken familial line. Thus, just as Chopin's text works to "name" Mamouche white, Mamouche's inherited surname finally allows Doctor John-Luis to locate his racial, ethnic, and class identity.

The long and spirited exchange that produces such information reveals that Mamouche is the grandson of two of the doctor's old acquaintances. Théodule Peloté, Mamouche's grandfather, is the handsome, fun-loving Cajun bachelor who was a favorite with the ladies, and Stéphanie Galopin is "the pretty Acadian girl" (*CW* 270) who married him. Bonner has suggested that Stéphanie was Doctor John-Luis's former love who ultimately rejected him in favor of Théodule,[19] and there is evidence early on in the story to support John-Luis's affection for Stéphanie. The mention of her name sets his "old head . . . fill[ing] with recollections" (CW 269), and later he remembers her as "the pretty Acadian girl, whom he had never wholly understood, even to this day" (CW 270). Thus, Stéphanie's choice of Théodule over Doctor John-Luis delineates differences between the two men's ethnic identities: Théodule, the carefree Cajun bachelor, had "never done a steady week's work in his life" (CW 270), while Doctor John-Luis, who went through school and built a medical practice, is now enjoying the fruits of his labor by living quite comfortably on his sizeable property.

However, as a moral for others who achieve prosperity through education and industry, Chopin writes of the doctor, "He might have owned a large plantation had he wished to own one, for a long life of persistent, intelligent work had left him with a comfortable fortune in his old age; but he preferred the farm on which he lived contentedly and raised an abundance to meet his modest wants" (CW 271).

Doctor John-Luis is neither greedy nor excessive with his acquired wealth but moderate in his preference for a relatively unadorned way of life. In this way he is neither the greedy, ruthless Creole of George Washington Cable's fiction, who drove his domestic servants and sharecroppers until they dropped;[20] nor is he the extravagant and vulgar type of nouveau-riche American, who, lacking genteel taste and experience with money, flaunts and squanders his wealth. Rather, Doctor John-Luis remains a quiet, dignified figure who prefers simple pleasures. He stands as an example of how the acquisition of wealth through appropriate means need not threaten or disrupt northern Anglo-Saxon power.

After Mamouche takes shelter from the rain and cold at Doctor John-Luis's house that night, Marshall informs the doctor the next morning that Mamouche is gone, and he reports the observations, "But de silver an' ev'thing dah; he ain't kiar' nuttin' off" (CW 271). Marshall's continued uncertainty about Mamouche's character draws from the language of racial discourse in his suspicions that Mamouche might have been a thief. But Doctor John-Luis, now fond of this grandson of his lost love, rejects any connections between Mamouche and criminality: "'Marshall,' snapped Doctor John-Luis, ill-humoredly, 'there are times when you don't seem to have sense and penetration enough to talk about! I think I'll take another nap,' he grumbled, as he turned his back upon Marshall. 'Wake me at seven'" (*CW* 271).

Although the Doctor's surly reply to Marshall issues a warning to readers that his fondness for Mamouche might be clouding his judgement, it is precisely his ability to feel affection for Mamouche that registers fundamental differences between this stranger and those who are more familiar to him. That Doctor John-Luis does not share those same feelings for the African Americans who have faithfully served and lived beside him for many years is indicated in an exchange between the doctor himself and his most intimate black employee: "'Marsh,' he said, 'you know, after all, it's rather dreary to be living alone as I do, without any companion — of my own color, you understand.' 'I knows dat, sah. It sho' am lonesome,' replied the sympathetic Marshall" (*CW* 272).

As one who is not the doctor's "own color," Marshall is marked as essentially different from the elite white Creole. His company and his words are not as important, satisfying, or valuable to Doctor John-Luis as those of other white folks. Though Marshall is worthy enough to fulfill temporarily the role of confidant and sympathizer, he is unsatisfactory as a permanent companion. In fact, he is not *even* a companion, as the doctor's qualified commentary ("without any companion — *of my own color*, you understand") makes clear.

However, beyond this anomaly of the capable Marshall, the rest of Doctor John-Luis's black help on the plantation are represented as abjectly inept. Such depictions work further to racialize African Americans by suggesting connections between biology and destiny. When Dr. John-Luis visits his orchard, where some workmen are planting fruit trees, he exclaims to himself, "'Tut, tut, tut!' They were doing it all wrong; the line was not straight; the holes were not deep. It was strange that he had to come down there and discover such things with his old eyes!" (*CW* 271). Impaired as his eyes are from age, Doctor John-Luis can nonetheless detect defects that his help "cannot."

Consequently, the strangeness that baffles Doctor John-Luis as to why he cannot trust his employees to do satisfactory work does not escape the reader. Chopin's message is that African Americans are a careless and unreliable inferior species whose subordinate status is predetermined. Although Doctor John-Luis is optimistic enough to believe otherwise, the text reinscribes African Americans' innate laziness and inevitable failure. When Doctor John-Luis pokes "his head into the kitchen to complain to Prudence about the ducks that she had not seasoned properly the day before, and to hope that the accident would never occur again" (*CW* 271), the narrative's inference makes clear to the reader that what the Doctor perceives as an irregular accident is a regular fact of life that will most definitely recur.

Only when Doctor John-Luis finally inspects the carpenter working on his fence do readers learn of the gate-tampering incident and of how a prankster has been unhooking various neighborhood gate hinges, wreaking havoc on local planters' farms by the freeing of farmers' livestock. As the doctor decides to offer a reward, he refers to the offense as both "provoking" and "malicious" (*CW* 271), words that come dangerously close to coding the act as criminal behavior. Thus, it is not merely coincidental that, when Mamouche is apprehended and brought before Doctor John-Luis as the perpetrator in the case, the question of Mamouche's character turns on the critical issue of whether he is a prankster or a thief:

> "Well, sir," interrupted the red-faced man [who caught Mamouche], "you've got a pretty square case against him, I see. Not only for malicious trespass, but of theft. See this bolt?" producing a piece of iron from his coat pocket. "That's what gave him away."
>
> "I en't no thief!" blurted Mamouche, indignantly. "It's one piece o' iron w'at I pick up in the road."
>
> "Sir," said Doctor John-Luis with dignity, "I can understand how the grandson of Théodule Peloté might be guilty of such mischievous pranks as this boy has confessed to. But I know that the grandson of Stéphanie Galopin could not be a thief." (*CW* 273–74)

By referencing Mamouche's grandparental heritage, Doctor John-Luis speaks the importance of lineage and the role heredity will play in Mamouche's ability to become culturally white. The fact that Théodule Peloté is Mamouche's grandfather accounts for his rascally male Cajun essence; the fact that his grandmother is Stéphanie Galopin speaks of his ability to overcome lower-class (Cajun) character deficits. By suggesting that virtuous white womanhood overrides mischievous manhood, Chopin's text conveniently elides class-bound definitions of femininity and in this way appropriates unimpeachable aristocratic southern femininity for Stéphanie and, consequently, her descendants.

Thus, when the reward is paid and Doctor John-Luis and Mamouche are alone together at last, it is Mamouche's grandmaternal heritage that made it seem "very good to Doctor John-Luis to have the boy sitting again at his fireside; and so natural, too. He seemed to him the incarnation of unspoken hopes; the realization of vague and fitful memories of the past" (CW 274).

Mamouche becomes not only the son Doctor John-Luis never had but also the specific son he had always hoped for: a son by Stéphanie Galopin. Bestowing tenderness upon Mamouche is tantamount to Doctor John-Luis's finally consummating his love for Stéphanie, so that even if Mamouche does not carry his blood, he nonetheless embodies the doctor's hopes and desires.

Consequently, the ideological purpose of Doctor John-Luis's arrested love story becomes clear when he proposes adoption as a means for uniting the doctor himself and Mamouche as a family: "'Mamouche,' [Doctor John-Luis] said, 'I want you to stay here; to live here with me always. To learn how to work; to learn how to study; to grow up to be an honorable man. An honorable man, Mamouche, for I want you for my own child'" (CW 274).

Doctor John-Luis's proposal to adopt Mamouche may be of a different kind from that of marriage, but his words constitute an admission of love, nonetheless. The incantatory effect of the preceding quotation, with its repetitive words and phrases, is poetic in quality, and so the text argues, such ardent, though romanticized parental love for this orphan boy can take place only if he is white.

However, although Mamouche's biological whiteness poses no obstacle to his inheriting Doctor John-Luis's white Creole name, Chopin's text makes it clear that Mamouche's consent to adopt bourgeois white values in return is also necessary for this marital-like integration to take place. To gain the social, financial, and material inheritance of ruling-class whiteness, Mamouche must undertake the work of acculturating himself to this higher, white(r) class.

Following this thinly veiled metaphor of romantic love, the story ends with a scene parallel to that of the first "morning after," when Mamouche chose to leave Doctor John-Luis after the latter had provided for his overnight accommodations. This time, however, when the doctor questions Marshall about Mamouche, Marshall responds, laughingly,

> "He kneelin' down dah on de flo'. He keep on sayin', 'Hail, Mary, full o' grace, de Lord is wid dee. Hail, Mary, full o' grace' — t'ree, fo' times, sah. I tell 'im, 'W'at you sayin' yo' prayer dat away, boy?' He 'low dat w'at his gran'ma larn 'im, ter keep outen mischief. W'en de devil say, 'Take dat gate offen de hinge; do dis; do dat,' he gwine say t'ree Hail Mary, an' de devil gwine tu'n tail an' run."
>
> "Yes, yes," laughed Doctor John-Luis. "That's Stéphanie all over."
>
> "An' I tell 'im: 'See heah, boy, you drap a couple o' dem Hail Mary, an' quit studyin' 'bout de devil, an' sot yo'se'f down ter wuk. Dat the oniest way to keep outen mischief.'"
>
> "What business is it of yours to interfere?" broke in Doctor John-Luis, irritably. "Let the boy do as his grandmother instructed him."
>
> "I ain't desputin', sah," apologized Marshall. (*CW* 274–75)

While Marshall openly mocks, and Doctor John-Luis affectionately smiles at the methods of Stéphanie's recommended remedy — methods whose efficacy northern Protestant readers, too, would have doubted — Doctor John-Luis does not allow Marshall to contradict her authority. Chopin's technique of placing northern Protestant doubt in a southern black body works brilliantly to undermine such criticism; in this way, she gives voice to northern objections but simultaneously undercuts them through Marshall's undervalued identity. However well-reasoned Marshall's commentary is, it is nonetheless derisively depicted in a nonstandard, uneducated, even comic black dialect. Clearly, Marshall's word is not the one readers are meant to heed in this story.

But the doctor's is, and it is Doctor John-Luis's words that readers hear at the end of the tale. Their invocation of the language of eugenics suggests the potential yet untapped in Mamouche: "'But you know, Marsh,' continued the doctor, recovering his usual amiability. 'I think we'll be able to do something with the boy. I'm pretty sure of it. For, you see, he has his grandmother's eyes; and his grandmother was a very intelligent woman; a clever woman, Marsh. Her one great mistake was when she married Théodule Peloté'" (*CW* 275).

While Mamouche is downstairs worshipping the Virgin Mother, Doctor John-Luis is upstairs paying homage to the ideal of southern white womanhood embodied in the memory of Stéphanie. Though Doctor John-Luis's thoughts reflect on the more physical and intellectual ways in which Mamouche resembles Stéphanie, those tangible traits are merely external signs of his less tangible moral and racial essence inherited from her. Stéphanie's typification of the goodness and purity embedded in the ideal of southern womanhood is the biological corrective for Cajun male devilishness. Though the text does not guarantee that Mamouche will reform, the critical issue for his white ethnic codification is that a promise of potential for growth be fundamentally present in the first place.

Like "Mamouche," "Polydore" also constructs Cajun ethnic identity as essentially different from blackness. Because black racial discourse from the most radically racist to the most liberally sympathetic worked to fix African Americans in one of two predetermined categories: (1) that of the fundamentally corrupt being for whom immorality was part of her or his nature; or (2) that of the essentially angelic creature whose innate, childlike innocence arrested his or her development, precluding that person from entering adulthood and/or becoming fully human,[21] Chopin colored Cajuns white through fictions of their potential ability to reform their ways and/or mature into responsible adults.

Thus, when Chopin begins "Polydore" with the sentence: "It was often said that Polydore was the stupidest boy to be found 'from the mouth of Cane river plumb to Natchitoches'"(*CW* 411), she immediately defends her character against any charges of racial dereliction by virtue of his gullibility. Simplemindedness, not incorrigibility, makes Polydore lie about his health to the entire plantation household. Though Chopin does not name the parties guilty of successfully "persuad[ing Polydore] . . . that he was an overworked and much abused individual" (*CW* 411), she acquits him of racial criminality through the assertion that it is the influence of others, not Polydore's own implacable immorality, that motivates his offense.

Of course, Polydore's plan of feigned illness backfires when his idleness directly causes the near death of his beloved godmother and guardian,

Illustration for "Polydore" printed in the *Youth's Companion*, New England edition, *The American Periodical Series on Microfilm*, 23 April 1896, page 214. Image published with permission of ProQuest Information and Learning Company. Further reproduction is prohibited without permission.

Mamzelle Adélaïde. When Polydore pleads lameness due to an imagined pain in his one leg, Mamzelle must run an errand in his stead in an open buggy under the sweltering, midday southern sun. Consequently, she suffers heat stroke and lies in bed for days, feverish and delirious. The overt moral to the story is that, if only Polydore had performed his apportioned duties within the family unit, all would have been well.

However, Chopin's tale accomplishes ideological work beyond this simple mandate to carry one's own weight, as it were, as a member of the family. Polydore's heartfelt remorse, confession, and repentance that follow act as signs of his moral development. Furthermore, they are penitence enough for Mamzelle, who, by the end of the story, accurately discerns that Polydore has come to love her as though she were his biological mother. Thus, when "she drew him close to her and kissed him as mothers kiss" (*CW* 417), Chopin's language of biology and family wholly recuperates Polydore as a white boy whose class-bound Cajun failing may be lower intelligence but is neither black racial delinquency nor arrested black development.

Chopin moderates Polydore's potential for innate racial villainy early on in the story by writing that, when he finally decided to pretend he was sick, "Polydore had formed no plan and had thought only vaguely upon results. He lay in a half-slumber awaiting developments, and philosophically resigned to any turn which the affair might take" (*CW* 411). Explained this way, Polydore's actions constitute less a premeditated offense than a childish prank whose perpetrator no more calculated his advantages if he succeeded than he considered his punishment if he failed. Thus, Polydore's mental density mitigates his culpability, since the advantage he would gain by tricking Mamzelle Adélaïde — his "motive" — is not clear even to him.

Unlike her treatment of Lolotte in "A Rude Awakening" or even Mamouche in the story by the same name, Chopin's signification of Polydore's white racial and Cajun ethnic identities is forthcoming. Readers first meet Polydore as a doted-on and wholly incorporated member of Mamzelle's bourgeois Creole family, an adopted son who enjoys the privileges of an upper-middle-class white child. Not only does Polydore sleep in the big house with Mamzelle Adélaïde and her father, old Monsieur José, but he has black servants at his beck and call. It is the black house menial Jude who first discovers Polydore's "illness" in the course of his round of morning wake-up calls, and it is Jude who answers Polydore's cowbell summons once the boy is believed to be ill.

Chopin's authorial voice even intercedes to explain how Polydore comes to inherit this comfortable Creole lifestyle: "[O]ne of the aims of Mamzelle Adélaïde's existence was to do the right thing by this boy, whose mother, a 'Cadian hill woman, had begged her with dying breath to watch over the temporal and spiritual welfare of her son; above all, to see that he did not follow in the slothful footsteps of an over-indolent father" (CW 412). Although historical records document that a minority of Cajuns achieved the coveted level of "planter class" and an even larger number married and engendered children with African Americans, Native Americans, and northern European Americans, Chopin's texts associate the term Cajun, which she spelled "'Cadian," exclusively with the white, economic underclass of French Canadian ancestry. This class difference that Chopin institutes to distinguish Cajuns from Creoles most obviously connotes economic disparity between the two groups, but it also, like racial discourse, comes dangerously close to articulating the *sociological* aspect of *socio*economic class difference through the language of biology as well. By the condescending description of Polydore's mother as a "'Cadian hill woman" and father as an "over-indolent" laborer, Chopin intimates that Polydore's intelligence — the only trait readers are told he inherits genetically from his parents — derives naturally from his class.

However, although Polydore's intellectual heredity is fixed, his moral behavior is not, so that Polydore remains a candidate for acculturation through his subscription to the honest industry of the Protestant work ethic. The realization Polydore comes to at the end of the text, "I know I can't he'p being stupid . . . but it's no call fo' me to be bad" (CW 417), iterates Polydore's essential difference from the racialized Negro in Chopin's texts. Polydore's disruptive behavior is a developmental stage that he will outgrow, not a permanent state of being that determines his lot for life.

In contrast, the fixedness of Chopin's African American characters in this text, namely Jude and Aunt Siney, is demonstrated by their stock characterization. While Jude is the uncomplaining, steadfast male servant, Aunt Siney is the farcical black cook whose African American dialect is drawn for comic effect. Aunt Siney's remedy of slathering bacon fat on Polydore's leg on a hot summer day in Louisiana, "de oniest way to draw out de misery" (*CW* 413), is laughable as much for its folk remedy as for its nonnecessity. Furthermore, her total and complete lack of authority within the plantation household is emphasized when she, "assuming a brief authority, forced [Polydore] to sit still by the kitchen door and talked further of bacon fat" (*CW* 414).

In stark comparison with both African Americans and Cajuns, the Creoles in "Polydore" are represented as regal and saintly. By writing that Mamzelle's "flowing muslin wrapper swept majestically from side to side as she walked" (*CW* 412), Chopin invokes the Creole's mythologized royal past, and by painting the virginal bridal and nunlike image of Mamzelle standing "beside the bed, lifting the mosquito bar that settled upon her head and fell about her like a veil" (*CW* 412), she references not only the sexual, but also the moral, purity of Mamzelle's virtuous white womanhood.

Class difference further enables Chopin to figure Mamzelle as a veritable angel who saves Polydore from the fate of class and racial descent, a "negroization" that would have befallen him had he stayed in his former environment. Chopin's text foreshadows Polydore's fate had Mamzelle not taken him in:

> There was a cabin up there on the hill that Polydore remembered well. Negroes were living in it now, but it had been his home once. Life had been pinched and wretched enough up there with the little chap. The bright days had been the days when his godmother, Mamzelle Adélaïde, would come driving her old white horse over the pine needles and crackling fallen twigs of the deserted hill-road. Her presence was connected with the earliest recollections of whatever he had known of comfort and well-being. (*CW* 414–15)

Thus, both Mamzelle Adélaïde and Monsieur José are represented in this text as being good through and through. When Polydore puts on his amateurishly executed act of limping and feeling pain, "His acting was clumsily overdrawn; and by less guileless souls than Mamzelle Adélaïde and her father would have surely been suspected. But these two only thought with deep concern of means to make him comfortable" (*CW* 413). Thus, it is not simply Mamzelle and Monsieur's ingenuousness that makes them worry after Polydore's well-being but, more significantly, their love and affection for him.

So out of concern for Polydore, Mamzelle Adélaïde, whose weight and age are beginning to compromise her own health, undertakes

> a long drive in the open buggy . . . a mission which would have fallen to Polydore had he not been disabled by this unlooked-for illness. She had thoughtlessly driven across the country at an hour when the sun was hottest, and now she sat panting and fanning herself; her face, which she mopped incessantly with her handkerchief, was inflamed from the heat. (*CW* 413–14)

Mamzelle's headache, delirium, and near-death that follow are classic symptoms of heat stroke, a malady that more readily befalls people of advancing age and weight, like Mamzelle, than younger folk, like Polydore. In spite of her symptoms, however, Polydore still hasn't connected Mamzelle's illness with its cause or understood his role in precipitating this current turn of events:

> Polydore did not think of these things in any connected or very intelligent way. They were only impressions that penetrated him and made his heart swell, and the tears well up to his eyes. He wiped his eyes on the sleeve of his night-gown. The mosquitoes were stinging him and raising great welts on his brown legs. He went and crept back under the mosquito-bar, and soon he was asleep and dreaming that his *nénaine* was dead and he left alone in the cabin upon the pine hill. (*CW* 415)

Up until this point, Polydore has been able to think only about himself, his pain, and his potential loss should Mamzelle Adélaïde die. However, when he hears Mamzelle apologizing to the specter of his deceased mother for her negligence in his care, suggesting that *she* was somehow responsible for the malady that affected his limb, Polydore begins to feel shame. Chopin's representation of Polydore slowly begins to change from that of immature prankster to mature and responsible son, so that his redeeming character trait is his ability to empathize with another. Instead of feigning illness, Polydore is now truly sick from worry, and it is that empathetic connection with his adoptive mother that enables him to hold himself accountable for her suffering:

> Polydore crouched on the gallery. It had finally come to him to comprehend the cause of his *nénaine*'s sickness — that drive in the sweltering afternoon, when he was shamming illness. No one there could have comprehended the horror of himself, the terror that possessed him, squatting there outside her door like a savage. If she died — but he could not think of that. It was the point at which his reason was stunned and seemed to swoon. (*CW* 416)

Polydore's recognition of his error, his willingness to take responsibility for his wrongdoing, and his conscious decision to emend his misbehavior are critical to his ability to become culturally white. Polydore thus absolves himself of his past sins the only way he knows how: He confesses his guilt to a priest and then confesses his confession to Mamzelle Adélaïde.

Per Seyersted notes that when the first serial printing of "Polydore" came out in the *Companion*, it was accompanied by a subtitle that summarized the story's plot thus: "Polydore. Two invalids, two confessions, and a penance. — A story of a stupid boy." The "two invalids" obviously refer to the one genuinely sick person in the tale, Mamzelle, and the one false one, Polydore; the "two confessions," to Polydore's initial admission to the priest and subsequent one to Mamzelle. The penance also may well have been spoken of in duplicate, since "penance" can signify either punishment or forgiveness, and Polydore had the former imposed on him by the Catholic Church and the latter offered by Mamzelle. However, Polydore's stupidity is singular, and though the serial title suggests it, the story does not end with his stupidity as an emphasis. The story instead ends with a poignant bonding between the repentant boy and the forgiving guardian, and the result is that the two learn to love each other in the most romanticized of nineteenth-century relationships, that between mother and child. In "Polydore," Chopin draws from contemporaneous motherhood and childhood lore to argue that, because of (white) woman's maternal nature and (white) children's eminent lovability, a beneficent Creole plantation mistress can love even as stupid a Cajun boy as Poly-dore. Her fiction offers one more piece of testimony to the period's belief that, through a (white) mother's love for a child, anything is possible.

4 Beyond Coloring Locals

After The Awakening, *"Charlie,"* *and Conventional Returns*

What happened to Chopin, her textual production, and her texts' marketability after the publication of *The Awakening* continues to be the subject of scholarly debate. Thus, I return in my conclusion to the point where I began in my introduction: revisiting yet another narrative surrounding this late nineteenth-century white bourgeois female author of Louisiana stories. Just as the identification of Chopin's agenda to "color locals"[1] has allowed us to revise several conclusions (for example, Chopin's fiction is notable for its ability to transcend its cultural milieu; white feminism is characteristic of her work; and Chopin wrote without regard to audience or publisher), this chapter in turn explores anew the long-standing question of what impact *The Awakening* had on the remainder of Chopin's life, career, and literary production and particularly why her subsequent texts became increasingly less concerned with either the politics of late nineteenth-century feminism or Creole and Cajun whitening.

But it will do so by examining evidence of Chopin's own sense, even if imagined, of her marketability following critical reviews of *The Awakening* rather than any "real" effect these reviews may have had on publishers.[2] Chief in this sequence of events is the curious fact that, between March 1899 and March 1900, the *Youth's Companion* bought, but never published, four of Chopin's short stories: "A Little Country Girl," "Alexandre's Wonderful Experience," "The Gentleman from New Orleans," and "A December Day in Dixie." As Toth has noted, the "*Youth's Companion* had bought stories from Kate Chopin before and not published them — but it was very unusual for a magazine to pay $150 in a year for stories it did not use" (Toth, *Kate Chopin* 373). However, precisely why the *Companion* elected not to publish these stories remains a matter of mere conjecture. For as Thomas has also documented, these tales were purchased around the time of *Companion* editor Daniel Ford's death in December 1899, leading Thomas to conclude that "in all likelihood these omissions [were] attributable to . . . a resultant change in editorial policy rather than any blacklisting of Chopin" (Thomas 49).

What is interesting to me is not whether the *Companion*'s new editorial guard thought Chopin too controversial a subject for its pages immediately following the publication of her novel or whether those stories purchased between March 1899 and March 1900 were misplaced or shoved aside in the temporary, yet undoubtedly hectic, time of transition between Ford and his successor. Instead, I am interested in how Chopin herself might have perceived the *Companion*'s editorial decisions and how these decisions affected her subsequent literary production and marketing strategies.

Of the four stories in question, only one — "A Little Country Girl" — was composed prior to *The Awakening*'s publication. The other three tales, "Alexandre's Wonderful Experience," "The Gentleman from New Orleans," and "A December Day in Dixie," were each written nearly a year after Chopin's novel had been circulating.[3] In addition to Thomas's observation that Chopin's post-*Awakening* fiction exhibits a new preoccupation with illness and death (resulting, she argues, from Chopin's own declining health), these texts are also more accommodationist in their gender politics for recognizably white women than Chopin's earlier stories.

Only "A December Day in Dixie" stands as an anomaly, as it is a reflective piece in the first person that hardly resembles Chopin's other fiction at all. However, in "Alexandre's Wonderful Experience," Chopin returns to her earlier, and thus safer, ethnic and class politics of assimilating an orphaned Creole youth into a white bourgeois household. By 1900, when the story was written, Chopin could have presumed, as she did in stories such as "Mamouche" and "Polydore," much less ideological resistance to fictions that colored Creoles and Cajuns white. Not only had Chopin been publishing for twelve years, but she was also in the literary company of popular Louisiana writers such as Grace King and Ruth McEnery Stuart, whose more emphatic Creole sympathies and radical racial politics encouraged in the popular imagination a receptivity to Chopin's more conservative own.

Furthermore, in "Alexandre's Wonderful Experience," Chopin deploys marriage and adoption as "rewards" for her characters' deserving behavior rather than as vehicles for social mobility that their ethnicity and/or class status would otherwise have prevented them from attaining. Alexandre does not need to be adopted by an upstanding white bourgeois couple in order to code him as white. Although Alexandre has long black hair, he speaks standard English, and his impeccable manners, solid work ethic, and moral sense, which is superior to that of his employer, are all made evident to the reader upon his very introduction in the text.

Similarly, the unnamed woman in black, whose marriage to the doctor brings about Alexandre's honesty and self-sacrifice, does not need her new husband's wealth to signify her status as a lady. Though her fortune is dwindling in her efforts to provide for her sick daughter, the unnamed woman has all of the refined speech, manners, and bearing of a thoroughly white, bourgeois background. Thus, everyone's improved economic status in the story is simply their just reward for internal characteristics that they already possess. Marriage in this tale functions as compensation, whereas in other stories about culturally intelligible white middle-class women, it is an institution Chopin readily critiques.

In "The Gentleman from New Orleans," Chopin enacts her white feminist politics by presenting a distressing picture of the wearing effect a controlling husband's behavior has on his wife. Though her critique of patriarchal authority stands, Chopin uncharacteristically softens it with a sentimental ending. Buddy Bénoîte, who has kept his in-laws off his property by the threat of his gun, is persuaded to relent when, after many years, Buddy's father-in-law comes to visit his estranged daughter and deliver news of her mother's impending death. Upon Buddy's witnessing the reunion between father and daughter, Chopin writes: "The sight of his wife's great emotion was a painful revelation. The realization that the tie which united those two clinging to each other out there was the same that bound his own to the cherished baby in his arms, was an overwhelming realization. His impulses were not slow. He hastened forward and held out his hand to his wife's father" (*CW* 636). Thus, Chopin's judgement against patriarchal authority in marriage is mitigated by Buddy's idealized reform.

Even Chopin's marketing strategies for these texts, along with others that were composed prior to *The Awakening* but marketed after its publication, show an unwillingness to risk rejection. Chopin solicited editors cautiously, sending her manuscripts only to those with whom she had had a successful track record. "A Little Country Girl," "Alexandre's Wonderful Experience," and "A December Day in Dixie" were all accepted by the *Youth's Companion* upon first submission. "The Gentleman from New Orleans" was offered first to the *Century* and, once rejected, was purchased by the *Companion*.[4] After *The Awakening*, then, Chopin not only wrote more conventional texts; her marketing practices were more tentative.

Two other tales written prior to but marketed after *The Awakening* appeared in a magazine Chopin did not often solicit. "The Godmother," written between January and February 1899, appeared in William Marion Reedy's St. Louis *Mirror* on 12 December 1901. Also, on 27 March 1902, the *Mirror* published "A Vocation and a Voice," a longer manuscript that was written in November 1896 and intended as the title story of Chopin's third and final volume of fiction by the same name.[5] Never before had Chopin solicited the *Mirror*, and on only one other occasion had a manuscript of hers been published in it, on request.[6] Chopin's play, "An Embarrassing Position. Comedy in One Act," appeared in the *Mirror* on 19 December 1895.

Just how calculating Chopin's decision to send her manuscripts to the *Mirror* was is indicated by her timing in soliciting its editor at this point in her career. Chopin had long been a friend of the *Mirror's* publisher, William "Billy" Reedy, who took over the weekly publication in 1893. Throughout Chopin's career, Reedy had publicly lavished praise on her work and had privately admired the woman herself, though to what degree their correspondences were mere flirtations even Toth is willing only to speculate (*Kate Chopin* 264–68).

Thus, Chopin was virtually guaranteed of Reedy's support many years before she called on it, and she might have used the *Mirror*, like *Vogue*, to showcase the unorthodox politics enacted in her more daring fiction. Under Reedy's guidance, the *Mirror* became renowned for its liberal stance in areas such as "society, politics, the arts, and sports and amusements" (Mott, vol. IV 653). Why Chopin never asked Reedy to publish one of her manuscripts before 1901 is unknown, but it is possible that the St. Louis-based weekly had not amassed the cultural cachet Chopin preferred of her publishers until the turn of the century, which even then was less than that of the older northeastern publications. Boasting a national circulation, the *Mirror* reached its zenith at roughly thirty thousand subscriptions in 1900, a trifle by comparison with other magazines in which Chopin had published, and though the magazine is remembered today for its support of new poetic and literary forms, famous names began appearing in the *Mirror* with regularity only about the time Chopin desired her work to be associated with it. As Mott has written of the magazine:

> Contributors to the *Mirror* during the twenty years beginning with 1898 make a fine list — which is much more impressive, however, in the second of the two decades. . . . In these months and years it was also publishing some of the work of Vachel Lindsay, Edwin Arlington Robinson, Carl Sandburg, and Robert Frost — a great quartet of a great period in Modern American poetry. (vol. IV 654)

Consequently, as a post-*Awakening* forum for her work, the *Mirror* suited Chopin's aims nicely. A hometown publication owned by a close friend, the *Mirror* allowed Chopin to capitalize on her local celebrity and make professional use of her personal contact. As a national publication associated with the literary avant-garde, the *Mirror* conferred the prestige she sought, and as a publication noted for its liberal politics, it offered her an expanded readership for those stories that she previously could have placed only with *Vogue*.[7]

The first two pieces Chopin wrote following *The Awakening* were completed in November 1899 and were never published. Though one of them, "A Reflection," has been categorized by more than one Chopin scholar as fiction, it more closely resembles Chopin's essays since it is without character or plot, two driving and essential elements of Chopin's fiction. A personal and philosophical piece about "fortunate beings" who "are born with a vital and responsive energy" and who "do [not] fall out of rank and sink by the wayside to be left contemplating the moving procession" (*CW* 622), Chopin never tried to place "A Reflection" with a publisher.

The second story, "Ti Démon," Chopin did attempt to place with some of the most prestigious periodicals of the day: the *Century*, *The Atlantic*, *Scribner's*, and the *Boston Brown Book*, all of whom rejected the manuscript. Ti Démon, the nickname that had once signified the boy's insufferably discontented infancy, "had lost all significance . . . in his growing goodness, and in the bovine mildness that characterized his youth years the name . . . became almost a synonym for gentleness" (*CW* 623). However, Ti Démon lives up to his namesake when, after drinking and gambling at his friend Aristides' urgings, Ti Démon later comes upon Aristides walking arm in arm with his fiancée, Marianne, and consequently flies into a rage, beating the notoriously suave Aristides senseless.

"Ti Démon" is the story of ethnic Cajun passion and the necessity of inculcating white Anglo-Saxon Protestant codes of restraint. However, if *The Atlantic*'s response is representative of the other periodicals Chopin solicited, "Ti Démon" was never published because, as Toth has noted, the story was deemed "'so sombre . . . the sad note seems to us too much accented to let us keep the story for the Atlantic'"(qtd. in *Kate Chopin* 362).

"CHARLIE"

In April 1900, exactly one year after *The Awakening* had been out, Chopin tried her hand at one last compromise tale about a recognizably white, bourgeois Creole girl's transformation into a woman. That story, "Charlie," focuses on the exploits of a tomboy daughter who eventually comes to occupy the traditional feminine roles of care-giver and helpmate to her ailing father, while she simultaneously — and unconventionally — takes on the role of plantation field manager in his stead. Chopin had reason to think her story would be acceptable to the "family values" press since her representation of a woman cross-dressing was not unusual for its time. Indeed, Barbara White demonstrates that Charlie's tomboyism and gender rebellion had American literary precedents (30 – 45). Thirteen-year-old Capitola "Cap" Black, in E.D.E.N. Southworth's *The Hidden Hand* (1849), saves a helpless young woman from kidnappers, engages in a duel, and dresses as a boy to find respectable work. Josephine "Jo" March, in Louisa May Alcott's *Little Women* (1868), holds on to her tomboyish youth as long as possible, even when sister Meg admonishes,

"You are old enough to leave off boyish tricks, and to behave better, Josephine" (qtd. in White 34). Like Southworth's Capitola Black, Magdaléna Yorba and Helena Belmont of Gertrude Atherton's *The Californians* (1898) get arrested for impersonating boys, and Kate Douglas Wiggin continues the tradition past Chopin's "Charlie" by representing fourteen-year-old Rebecca Rowena of *Rebecca of Sunnybrook Farm* (1903) as preferring boys' activities to girls'.

By charting the existence of these rebellious heroines in sentimental novels, White establishes a nineteenth-century American literary tradition of young female heroines who antedate those in "bonafide" novels of adolescence in the 1920s.[8] Characterizing these early novels' similarity as their sustained interest in a young female's entrance into gendered adulthood, White documents a discursive history of conflict over gendered identity in which a female's androgynous freedom is tolerated only in her youth.

"Charlie," Chopin's novella about a seventeen-year-old girl whose masculine nickname inspires the story's title, clearly participates in this tradition.[9] Charlotte "Charlie" Laborde is the second eldest of seven sisters, all of whom have managed on their Louisiana plantation with their father and a school mistress since the death of their mother. Charlie is the tomboy of the lot, who, in her rebellion against gender prescriptions, "wore a costume of her own devising, something between bloomers and a divided skirt which she called her 'trouserlets.' Canvas leggings, dusty boots and a single spur completed her costume" (*CW* 639).

Charlie has an especially close relationship with her father, Mr. Laborde, who, "upon the point of separation from any of his daughters . . . had set his heart with stubborn determination" (*CW* 643). However, Charlie's cross-gendered behavior also results from her devoted father's clandestine delight in her transgressive gender ways: "Charlie could ride and shoot and fish; she was untiring and fearless. In many ways she filled the place of that ideal son he had always hoped for and that had never come" (*CW* 644).

Charlie's involvement with her father lends itself to being read according to psychosocial interpretations of Freudian psychoanalytic discourse. By recasting Freud's psychosexual narratives as psychosocial ones, poststructuralist feminist scholars have appropriated Freudian language and deployed it not as a *pre*scription of the way gender development ought to take place but as a *de*scription of how gender becomes manifest in nuclear family dramas of the Western world.[10] Thus, because Charlie "really felt that nothing made much difference so long as her father was happy; [h]er actions were reprehensible in her own eyes only so far as they interfered with his peace of mind" (*CW* 643), Charlie follows what Freudian psychoanalytic discourse articulates as the "normal" path to femininity, insofar as "normalcy" is dictated by the daughter's conformity to the father's desires. In her verve to please her father, Charlie fashions her identity to satisfy his dual desire for both a daughter and a son and, as such, becomes precisely what her father desires her to be.[11] Thus, in "Charlie," Chopin imagines a psychosocial family drama wherein the father approves of his daughter's transgressive gender behavior.

However, Chopin makes evident how the Laborde family patriarch's desires are not consistent with those of a more dominant, conservative, and ubiquitous American patriarchal culture. Neither Charlie's (northern) governess, Miss Melvern, nor her (southern) Aunt Clementine — two conventional "ladies" who have followed standard paths to femininity — can persuade Mr. Laborde to inculcate in Charlie exclusively female gender norms, until she accidently wounds a young man by the name of Firman Walton in a target-practicing incident. Mr. Laborde's reluctant decision to send Charlie to a ladies' finishing school after this offense — his halfhearted attempt at reforming her errant (gender) ways — is not so repugnant to the girl as it once might have been, for she not only wants to please her father but is now enamored with the thought of entertaining young Walton as a suitor and thus wishes to become proficient at cultivating the feminine arts.

Charlie's easy acceptance of this landmark occasion in her life when she is expected to "become" a woman is explained by her classic psychosocial development in regard to her relationship with her father. In desiring to please Walton, Charlie demonstrates that she has transferred her culturally unacceptable desire for her father onto a culturally acceptable male other who can provide for her the (Freudian) all-important son. By following this, Freud's standard path to femininity, Charlie further demonstrates that she presumes she is meeting her father's expectations for her: to move on from her originary nuclear family and start a family of her own.

Freud's psychosexual account of how the daughter is "seduced" to leave her parents' family in order to satisfy her ultimate desire (for babies) intersects with the social in its reliance upon the marital romance plot, the culturally instituted story of how men fall in love with and marry women. Charlie's quite literal engagement with this romance fiction is evident by her insistence upon wearing her deceased mother's engagement ring even when she is at home sporting boys' clothing. The cherished heirloom, and Charlie's identification with her mother through it, bespeaks Charlie's ideological entrenchment in a patriarchal system that signifies white, middle-class woman as the beautiful, passive object to her complement: the strong, active male subject. Thus, young, single women, according to this cultural script, are valued primarily in terms of their marriageability, their worth as commodified objects, whose degree of decorativeness determines their odds for attracting a husband.

The text of "Charlie" emphasizes this social aspect of Charlie's gender development in its representation of gender as a cultural construct. Through Charlie's dual — and exaggerated — masculine and feminine behaviors, Chopin exposes gender to have no ontological origin at all but rather to be the effect of signifying practices, what Judith Butler has described as a performance, a "stylization of the body."[12] While at the seminary, Charlie is just as dramatic a young "woman" as she was a "boy." Acting her feminine part to excess, Charlie does not learn the delicate artistry of a selective curl in her hair; rather, she twists every strand until her head looks "like a prize chrysanthemum" (CW 657). Charlie's tastes are equally indulgent in her way of dress: "She wanted lace and embroideries upon her garments; and she longed to bedeck herself with ribbons and passementeries which the shops displayed in such tempting arrary" (CW 656).

By the end of her stay at the seminary, Charlie is able to give an acceptable performance of culturally intelligible femininity. She relishes these accomplishments, as we learn when her father visits the seminary and takes her for a day out. Entrenched in their respective father/daughter roles, the reunion plays out the Freudian script of the daughter's seduction by the father, while that seduction properly stays within the boundaries of the implicitly understood incest taboo:[13]

> [W]hen her father came alone one morning quite early — he had remained over night in the city that he might be early — and carried her off with him for the day, her delight knew no bounds. He did not tell her in so many words how hungry he was for her, but he showed it in a hundred ways. He was like a school boy on a holiday; it was like a conspiracy; there was a flavor of secrecy about it too. They did not go near Aunt Clementine's. . . .
>
> They went to the lake to eat breakfast; a second breakfast to be sure, but such exceedingly young persons could not be expected to restrict themselves to the conventional order in the matter of refreshment. . . . Their small table was out where the capricious breeze beat about them, and they sat looking across the glistening water, watching the slow sails and feeling like a couple of bees in clover. (*CW* 661–62)

The "romance" evident in the preceding passage continues as Charlie attempts to please her father with her hard-won feminine likenesses. However, consistent with Freudian psychoanalytic discourse, the seduction stays within bounds of the incest taboo, and so Charlie's and her father's flirtations remain just that. In a scene in which Charlie tries to live up to her elder sister Julia's exemplary feminine legacy, her father, whose unorthodox desires for Charlie, his favorite (tomboy) daughter, warns against putting too much stock in frivolous (feminine) pursuits. Extending her hand to her father, Charlie says:

> "Feel that. You know what it used to be. Ever feel anything softer than that?"
>
> He held the hand fondly in both of his, but she withdrew it, holding it at arm's length.
>
> "Now, dad, I want your candid opinion; don't just say anything you don't believe; but do you think it's as white as — Julia's for instance?"
>
> He narrowed his eyes, surveying the little hand that gleamed in the sun, like a connoisseur sizing up a picture.

"I don't want to be hasty," he said quizzically. "I'm not too sure that I remember, and I shouldn't like to do Julia's hand an injustice, but my opinion is that yours is whiter."

She threw an arm around his neck and hugged him, to the astonishment of a lame oysterman and a little Brazilian monkey that squealed in his cage with amusement.

"It's all right, Charlie dear, but you know you mustn't think too much about the hands and all that. Take care of the head, too, and the temper." (*CW* 662)

Despite her father's sensible advice, advice that he as easily might have given to a son as to a daughter, Charlie continues to engage with the marital romance plot, as indicated by her efforts to please young Walton. Even when Mr. Laborde's tragic sugar mill accident severs his arm and forces Charlie home from school, she keeps up the feminine practices of dress and grooming she has learned at the seminary, precisely because Walton has become a regular visitor at the plantation.

Charlie's journey toward femininity derails, however, when the rewards that the marital romance plot promises never come to be. Firman Walton proposes marriage not to Charlie but instead to Julia, and it is at the discovery of this event that Charlie discards her dress, dons her trouserlets, and takes her epiphanous horse ride. Afterward, Charlie is significantly changed:

> In her mad ride Charlie had thrown off the savage impulse which had betrayed itself in such bitter denunciation of her sister. Shame and regret had followed and now she was steeped in humiliation such as she had never felt before. She did not feel worthy to approach her father or her sisters. The girlish infatuation which had blinded her was swept away in the torrents of a deeper emotion, and left her a woman. (*CW* 667)

Charlie's transformation that has taken place in this passage is the significant turning point in the establishment of her identity; the experience has "left her a woman." The context in which Chopin places the signifier "left" suggests that Charlie somehow has been cleansed and that the contaminant that was swept away was her girlish infatuation for Firman Walton. Thus, Charlie repudiates the marital romance script and instead locates her womanhood in her responsibility and commitment to her originary nuclear family.

The height of Charlie's epiphany is indicated in her language the next morning when she sees her father and confesses she's been "climbing a high mountain" and that she "saw the new moon" (*CW* 667). Charlie no longer "engages" with the marital romance plot, as indicated when she gives her mother's formerly cherished ring to Julia "inconsequentially" (*CW* 668). By giving up her engagement with the cultural plot of romance that would have her enact the psychosocial transfer of her desire for her father onto another, Charlie becomes temporarily staid in her psychosocial development and thus becomes all the more "engaged" with her father.[14] What was once a quasi-symbiotic relationship becomes total symbiosis, when Charlie proposes that she supplant Gus Bradley as her father's substitute field manager, and it is here that Chopin has Charlie take advantage of the opportunities that Chopin, the author, has arranged for her: "'I'm jealous of Mr. Gus,' [Charlie] said. 'I know as much as he, more perhaps when it comes to writing letters. I know as much about the plantation as you do, dad; you know I do. And from now on I'm going to be — to be your right hand — your poor right hand'" (*CW* 667–68).

Charlie's situation described in the preceding passage is both liberating and confining — liberating because Chopin imagines a world in which Charlie can occupy the masculine sphere of business and commerce as a woman, confining because that occupancy comes at a price: Charlie must remain the dutiful daughter. Through metonymic displacement, the substitution of her hand for his, Charlie acquires her father's authority by proxy, an unmediated access to the power of his word. Dressing as a male, having male power, and inhabiting the male sphere, Charlie returns to the androgyny of her youth, although her masculine freedoms are checked by her feminine familial responsibilities. As long as her disabled father lives, she is forever bound by her roles as helpmate and caregiver to him.

Not surprisingly, then, Chopin's ending merely flirts with the possibility of Charlie's eventually moving on from her responsibilities to her father and marrying another man. Late one evening Charlie's long-time admirer, Gus Bradley, says to her:

> "There's something I wanted to ask you."
> "I know. You want to ask me not to call you 'Mr.' Gus any more."
> "How did you know?"
> "I am clairvoyant. And besides you want to ask me if I like you pretty well."
> "You *are* clairvoyant!"
> "It seems to me I've always liked you better than any one, and that I'll keep on liking you more and more. So there! Good night." She ran lightly away into the house and left him in an ecstasy in the moonlight. (*CW* 669)

This unfinished ending of Charlie's flirtation with Gus leaves open the possibility that she may one day become the reproductive wife. However, by having Charlie choose Gus, Chopin amends the traditional marital romance script. Gus does not objectify Charlie by loving her for her passive beauty but, rather, appreciates all of her active, cross-gendered ways. Furthermore, in her role as plantation field manager, Charlie is the boss and Gus is the employee, and the more entrenched Charlie's power becomes on the plantation, the less chance that power has of being eroded by the traditional subordination of wife to husband.

However, this progressive marriage is presumably sometime off in the future, for Charlie can never "disengage" with her father as long as he is alive. Even though Chopin leaves open the possibility of Charlie's marrying Gus, that possibility is undercut by Mr. Laborde's continued presence, which Charlie is reminded of at the very moment when she leaves her suitor:

> "Is that you, Charlie?" asked her father at the sound of her light footfall. She came and took his hand, leaning fondly over him as he lay in the soft, dim light.
> "Did you want anything, Dad?"
> "I only wanted to know if you were there." (*CW* 670)

By choosing to have Mr. Laborde's words end her tale, Chopin authors the compromise that *The Awakening* lacked and without which, I would argue, she feared her text would not be marketable. Chopin reconciles Charlie's newly acquired masculine power with conventional gender ideology by limiting her freedom. The only masculine sphere Charlie can inhabit is intimately tied to her feminine one, which obliges her to maintain the traditional, self-sacrificing role of care-giver to her familial dependents.

Significantly, woman's obligations to others are what Edna Pontellier flees from in *The Awakening*, both throughout the novel and at its very end. Just as Edna says regarding motherhood early in the novel, that "I would give up the unessential; I would give my money, I would give my life for my children; but I wouldn't give *myself*" [emphasis added] (*CW* 929), so Ivy Schweitzer reads Edna's suicide at the novel's end as her attempt to "[give] birth to herself as a creature which has become its own mother" (Schweitzer 163). Like Sandra Gilbert and Susan Gubar's well-known assertion that Edna's drowning constitutes a mythic transcendence beyond culture, Schweitzer argues that Chopin's novel constructs a utopian vision that frees Edna from the confines of gender ideology.[15]

Both Schweitzer's and Gilbert and Gubar's arguments suggest an important connection between *The Awakening* and "Charlie." That is, if *The Awakening* constitutes Chopin's fictionalized, utopian answer to The Woman Question, "Charlie" is its realistic counterpart, Chopin's attempt to imagine a compromise that enables the female self to survive by expanding her power in the social world. "Charlie" is the imaginative rendering of Edna's story before Edna enters the ideological traps of marriage and motherhood; it is a revisionist writing of *The Awakening*'s white feminist politics, even if those politics can be enacted within culture only in a limited way and through a Creole woman.

More than noteworthy is the fact that Chopin's choice of "Charlie" for her main character's nickname is far more American than her first choice, "Jacques." Chopin's text was originally titled "Jacques," as she had named her main character Jacqueline "Jacques" Laborde. Chopin's handwritten manuscript at the Missouri Historical Society confirms that approximately one-third of the text was fully drafted before Chopin renamed "Jacques" as "Charlie." Chopin's choice to further Anglicize this Creole character through her nickname suggests Chopin's desire to have the text of "Charlie" be part of the ongoing dialogue regarding *The Awakening* and its main character, Edna, an upper-middle-class Kentucky Protestant. As McCullough has already noted, Edna's gender transgressions proved to be offensive precisely because they were committed by a white Anglo-Saxon Protestant woman. Embodying defiance in the Creole Charlotte Laborde suggests Chopin's desire to "have it both ways": to keep *The Awakening*'s themes part of the public debate through Charlie and to defend herself from further public rebuke through Charlotte.

Chopin must have thought her identity politics in "Charlie" were conventional enough, for she sent the manuscript to the *Youth's Companion* and the *Century*, two of the period's premiere family periodicals whose political agendas Chopin knew well, since she had placed much of her fiction with them. However, both magazines promptly rejected the manuscript, and there is nothing in Chopin's private papers that helps to explain why.[16] Though Chopin attempts to reconcile her feminism with conventional gender ideology in "Charlie," we must assume that the manuscript was unilaterally rejected because she did not satisfy her editors in this regard. Chopin's other compromise texts composed in 1900 — "Alexandre's Wonderful Experience," "The Gentleman from New Orleans," and "A December Day in Dixie" — were at least purchased by the *Companion*, even if they were not published.

Unlike those of her literary antecedents Jo, Magdaléna, and Helena, Charlie's gender transgression is not definitively reined in by marriage or, more significantly, by her exclusive subscription to woman's traditional place.[17] In *All-American Girl: The Ideal of Real Womanhood in Mid-Nineteenth-Century America*, Frances B. Cogan explains how crucial this maintenance of separate spheres was for mid-to-late-nineteenth-century women who desired extended power and autonomy for themselves. Cogan argues that the "reformers" who were successful in acquiring those freedoms did so by articulating them *as part of* woman's customary domain so as not to encounter substantial cultural resistance.

Cogan identifies this tenable, early feminist sentiment as a coherent movement that she calls "the ideal of Real Womanhood," an ideal that she claims self-consciously competed against the Cult of True Womanhood on the one hand and what Real Womanhood supporters viewed as more aberrant expressions of androgynous equality (the later New Woman, whom opponents dubbed the "Mannish Lesbian")[18] on the other:

The ideal of the Real Woman was a popular, middle-of-the-road image that recognized the disparities and the dangers protested by early
feminists but tried to deal with those ugly realities in what it saw as
a "female" way. It placed itself, therefore, firmly in the "separate
sphere" controversy by claiming a unique sphere of action and duty
for women, but one vastly extended and magically swollen past the di-
mensions of anything meant by that term to devotees of competing
True Womanhood. (4)

Although Cogan dates the ideal of the Real Woman from 1840 to 1880,
claiming it "dissolved, because it could no longer resist the contradictory
tensions pulling it toward resolution either into the conservative camp of
True Womanhood or into the growing tide of turn-of-the-century feminism" (257), Susan Tucker's excellent reading of young women's scrapbooks written between 1880 and 1918 confirms that the cultural practice
of allowing women to experience expanded freedoms — as long as those
freedoms were accommodated to women's traditional roles — continued
into the twentieth century. As Tucker argues, young college women of
this period recorded their accomplishments in academics and sports and
then re-coded these achievements as training for their expected "careers"
in life: those of wife and mother.[19]

Thus, Chopin's "Charlie" is most subversive in its representation of
a woman — even a Creole woman — acquiring unfettered authority
as plantation manager within the decidedly masculine sphere. Although
Chopin attempts to mitigate Charlie's newly acquired power by chaining
her to a lifelong obligation to her father, her textual politics must have
been unacceptable to her editors. As Seyersted has said, "Charlie," like
The Awakening, is the story of "a woman taking the liberties of a man"
(183), and so it is highly possible that these texts were each objectionable
to editors on similar grounds.

CONVENTIONAL RETURNS

I believe it is entirely possible that the rejection of "Charlie" by
the Companion and the Century, along with the Companion's willingness
to purchase, but unwillingness to publish, four of Chopin's stories the
previous year led to the even more conservative impulses we find in her

subsequent literary production and marketing beyond those she had put into practice immediately following *The Awakening*. In her desire to regain her literary currency, Chopin not only turned exclusively to her most supportive publishers but also sent them the type of fiction that she was virtually certain they would accept. Chopin thus returned to *Vogue* for the placement of a sad tale about a woman whose life never quite took flight. "The White Eagle," whose composition was completed on 9 May 1900, was accepted by *Vogue* upon first submission and was printed just two months later on 12 July. Though the story does not address issues of female sexuality, it does offer a critique of woman's place in society; and Chopin presumably chose *Vogue* because she wanted to see her tale published where it was sure to be sympathetically received.[20]

However, the textual politics in the two stories written after "Charlie" — "The Wood-Choppers" and "Polly" — are not compromise tales at all; in fact, they are diametrically opposed to Chopin's bold feminist politics in *The Awakening*, even though they feature young, eligible white female characters facing marriage proposals, materials that heretofore provided Chopin with the fodder for trenchant cultural critique.[21] Chopin takes no chance with editors objecting to these stories on moral grounds, for without even the objective of "coloring locals" to mediate her deployment of femininity, she uncharacteristically retreats from the opportunity to expose female oppression in late nineteenth-century gender ideology, resolving her characters' dilemmas instead through the traditional marriage plot.[22]

That "The Wood-Choppers" and "Polly" are entirely orthodox in their resolutions of The Woman Question for culturally intelligible white female characters becomes readily apparent when they are read against an earlier *Companion* text, one whose main character is also a young white female and one whose richly ambiguous ending contains nuances of the white feminist sentiment for which Chopin is typically celebrated.[23] That story is "Aunt Lympy's Interference," published in the *Youth's Companion* on 12 August 1897.

"Aunt Lympy's Interference" is the story of Melitte De Broussard, a Creole daughter of the slave-holding South, whose parents' deaths after the war leave her and her brother with little inheritance. Melitte, who "did not fully realize that her surroundings were poor and pinched" (*CW* 515)

Illustration for "Aunt Lympy's Interference" printed in the *Youth's Companion*, New England edition, *The American Periodical Series on Microfilm*, 12 August 1897, page 373. Image published with permission of ProQuest Information and Learning Company. Further reproduction is prohibited without permission.

takes satisfaction in her simple life and, as we meet her in the story, has recently "been conducting a small school which stood down the road at the far end of the Annibelle place" (*CW* 511). With her small bit of independent income, Melitte lives quite sufficiently with her brother and sister-in-law and their three young children.

The conflict of the story begins when Aunt Lympy, a former De Broussard slave who was Melitte's mammy, discovers that her former young mistress "was turn school-titcher" (*CW* 513). Aunt Lympy is (stereotypically) aghast and dismayed at what Melitte's employment suggests about this daughter of a once great southern family, and so she "interferes" by writing Melitte's wealthy, maternal uncle in New Orleans. The uncle responds appropriately, inviting Melitte to come and live with him and his daughters, "who were quite as eager to call her 'sister' as he was desirous of subscribing himself always henceforward, her father" (*CW* 513). Melitte's family, her neighbors, and even her little pupils become so obsessed with the fantasy of Melitte living the life of a society belle that they take for granted she will go — although Melitte is not so sure that she will.

Chopin uses Melitte's ambivalence about her departure to comment on widely held cultural assumptions about female desire — what women want out of life. Uncle Gervais's proposal constitutes for Melitte not only a material relocation of place but a metaphorical one in the social hierarchy as well. Although everyone around Melitte cannot imagine a young woman giving up this opportunity to be so securely (and stylishly) provided for, part of Melitte's reluctance to accept her uncle's offer has to do with her desire for independence and self-sufficiency. When Uncle Gervais "sent her a sum of money to supply her immediate wants" (*CW* 513), Melitte "put the money carefully aside to return to her uncle. She would in no way get it confounded with her own small hoard; that was something precious and apart, not to be contaminated by gift-money" (*CW* 514). In these lines Chopin contrasts Melitte's appreciation for honestly earned money with her disdain for "gift-money," which feels to her like stolen goods that she possesses unethically.

Melitte is equally reluctant to close down her school. Weeks after receiving Uncle Gervais's letter, Melitte holds fast to her daily routine of conducting classes. Melitte's sister-in-law's advice, that "'it's time you were dismissing an' closing up that school of yo's, Melitte,'" (*CW* 514–15) falls on deaf ears, as Melitte "did not answer. She seemed to have been growing sullen and ill-humored since her great piece of good luck; but perhaps she did not hear, with the pink sunbonnet covering her pink ears" (*CW* 515). Chopin makes clear, however, that Melitte's biggest reason for not wanting to leave home is her "strong attachment for the things about her — the dear, familiar things. . . . The thought of entering upon a different existence troubled her" (*CW* 515). Melitte clearly wants to be appreciated by those around her, to know that she's wanted and loved. She asks her brother's children, who also "were bitten with this feverish ambition for Melitte's worldly advancement. . . . 'Then you want *ti tante* to go away an' leave you all?'" (*CW* 514).

Additionally, she inwardly questions:

> Why was every one, with single voice, telling her to "go"? Was it that no one cared? She did not believe this, but chose to nourish the fancy. It furnished her a pretext for tears.
>
> Why should she not go, and live in the ease, free from responsibility and care? Why should she stay where no soul had said, "I can't bear to have you go, Melitte?"
>
> If they had only said, "I shall miss you, Melitte," it would have been something — but no! Even Aunt Lympy, who had nursed her as a baby, and in whose affection she had always trusted — even she had made her appearance and spent a whole day upon the scene, radiant, dispensing compliments, self-satisfied, as one who feels that all things are going well in her royal possessions. (*CW* 515)

Ultimately, it is Victor Annibelle, Melitte's admirer from the nearby plantation, who begs her not to leave when he expresses his deep and long-held love for her. Chopin ends her narrative thus:

> So after all Melitte did not go to the city to become a *grande dame*. Why? Simply because Victor Annibelle asked her not to. The old people when they heard it shrugged their shoulders and tried to remember that they, too, had been young once; which is, sometimes, a very hard thing for old people to remember. Some of the younger ones thought she was right, and many of them believed she was wrong to

sacrifice so brilliant an opportunity to shine and become a woman of fashion.

Aunt Lympy was not altogether dissatisfied; she felt that her interference had not been wholly in vain. (*CW* 517)

Like that in "Charlie," Chopin's ending in "Aunt Lympy's Interference" merely flirts with the possibility of Melitte marrying, leaving readers to imagine what happens between Melitte and Victor beyond what Chopin tells us. But unlike "Charlie," a text composed after *The Awakening*, the ending in "Aunt Lympy's Interference" is not a qualified one but, rather, one open-ended enough to suggest more than a single possible outcome. On the one hand, Chopin's text strongly points toward the certainty that Melitte and Victor will marry. The story ends with: (1) Victor professing his love for Melitte; (2) Melitte refusing to leave home "simply because Victor asked her not to"; (3) old townspeople remembering the power of youthful romance; and (4) Aunt Lympy satisfied that her interference has "provided for" Melitte after all.

On the other hand, to claim that Melitte and Victor's marriage is certain is also to read things into the text that are not there. Even though the townspeople and Aunt Lympy clearly believe Melitte refused Uncle Gervais's proposal because she intends to marry Victor, Chopin never lets Melitte articulate her reasons for doing so but rather lets readers infer Melitte's intentions, and there are inferences earlier in the text that suggest that Melitte did not refuse her uncle in order to marry Victor.

Throughout the story Melitte desperately wants someone, anyone, to entreat her to stay, and so we can assume that such entreaties by her brother's children or school pupils would have had the same effect on her as Victor's. To read the ending as confirmation of a marriage is to ignore Melitte's commitment to her school, her satisfaction in her independence, and her "strong attachment for the things about her." I read "Aunt Lympy's Interference," then, as a decidedly feminist text in its refusal to be pinned down to a conventional ending. It is not a text that accommodates its progressive gender politics to a more conservative mentality but rather one that defies a definitively conservative reconciliation.

However, the potentially subversive feminist moments in "The Wood-Choppers" and "Polly" are wholly recuperated by orthodox gender politics. Seyersted has written of the two heroines in each text, saying that "Léontine and Polly—both hold positions (one as a teacher, the other as a bookkeeper); but they are more than happy to marry and exchange their work for the 'labor of loving' which Paula von Stoltz [in "Wiser Than a God"], Mrs. Chopin's early heroine, had refused" (*Critical Biography* 185). So conventional is "The Wood-Choppers" that it is Chopin's only formulaic North-South reconciliation text, one that involves the standard portrayal of a poor-but-genteel southern young lady marrying a wealthy-but-rough-around-the-edges northern man. Chopin's mark of authorial individuality in using the North-South reconcilation theme comes from her representing her bride-to-be as a Louisiana Creole and the bride's intended as an American, who speaks only one language — English — to his fiancée's more sophisticated bilingualism in English and French.

The story begins with Léontine, a young, white schoolteacher, deciding to release her pupils from class early one day because of the season's torrential downpours. She returns to her "poor little bit of a Southern house" (*CW* 674) where she and her elderly mother live together, only to find the feeble woman bent "at the fireplace scraping together a few red ashes between the andirons" (*CW* 675). Angry that the local black and Cajun men did not come as promised to chop wood for them and dismayed at the thought of her mother suffering through the cold weather without a fire, Léontine takes the ax herself and begins chopping firewood.

In Léontine, Chopin draws the picture of a defiant young woman who is willing to provide for herself when no one else will. But Léontine's potential as a radically subversive figure is interrupted early in the story when Chopin, subsuming her character's masculine behavior within some acceptable form of femininity, addresses her readers directly, saying "Léontine was what they sometimes, in that region, call 'spunky'" (*CW* 676). This "spunky" (as opposed to aberrant) young woman becomes progressively more orthodox as the text progresses, and by the end she is recognizable as a bourgeois True Woman who no longer needs to chop her own wood or earn her own money in order to live comfortably.

When Léontine is outside in the rain unsuccessfully attempting to split wood, her new American (read: white, Anglo-Saxon) neighbor, George Willet, happens by and insists on taking over the task for her. Mr. Willet is a wealthy plantation owner who has the manly American habit of speaking

Illustration for "The Wood-Choppers" printed in the *Youth's Companion*, New England edition, *The American Periodical Series on Microfilm*, 29 May 1902, page 270. Image published with permission of ProQuest Information and Learning Company. Further reproduction is prohibited without permission.

in casual phrases. "'Pardon me, ladies,'" [Willet] said, with an easy inclination. 'My name's Willet. I live six miles below here — Slocum place.
Just want to be neighborly'" (*CW* 677). He also harbors a hearty dose of
racial prejudice, evident when he jokes with Melitte, "'Are the men Indi-
ans in this parish, that they let the women chop wood?'" and "'Isn't there
any black fellow around these diggings to chop your wood?'" (*CW* 676).

Brazen and direct though he may be in manner, however, Willet is
soft and refined at heart. He courts Léontine indirectly by leaving gifts
of food at her doorstep and apparently offers to pay local men willing to
perform custodial chores for the women because, "for some mysteri-
ous cause, [these men] fairly fought with each other over the privilege
of chopping wood and rendering themselves generally useful about the
place" (*CW* 678).

Furthermore, Chopin does not choose to have Léontine stubbornly
resist Willet's attentions but rather portrays her as succumbing to them
rather easily and even defends her for doing so:

> When [Willet] called one Sunday afternoon, having obtained [Léon-
> tine's] mother's permission to do so, [Léontine] was at first the small
> personification of dignity and reserve. This time he had brought a book
> with him, and some magazines, and the girl, hungry for such things,
> must have been of stone not to have melted somewhat under this be-
> nign influence. (*CW* 678)

In fact, Léontine's only worry is that Willet's kindness toward her and her
mother is merely in the spirit of neighborliness instead of romance:

> Once she said, with great show of emotion:
> "Mother, you must put a stop to Mr. Willet's constant visits and at-
> tentions. Some day he will be bringing a wife home to his plantation.
> Some one who may look down on us, who will be disagreeable, whom
> we will dislike. I'm *sure* we will dislike her. Such men always marry
> women whom people dislike!" (*CW* 678)

But only a short paragraph later Léontine and Willet alight from the
planter's buggy to announce to Léontine's mother their engagement. The
happy couple then moves into Willet's sizeable estate after the wedding,

and Chopin writes that "there was but one of Léontine's possessions that George Willet laid personal claim to. That was the heavy old ax. He bore it away himself in a sort of triumph, proclaiming that as long as he lived it should hold a place of honor in his establishment" (*CW* 679).

Late twentieth-century students who have read the body of Chopin's work and who have come to appreciate it primarily for its feminist sentiments will find it tempting to read this ending as Willet's valuing Léontine for her independence. However, the word of the text belies this story's easy categorization as a subversive document. First, at no other time does Léontine exhibit the "spunkiness" of her early wood-splitting incident, and second, that incident, in which Léontine exhibited unladylike behavior, "seemed by mutual consent to be eliminated from their conversation" (*CW* 678). The spectacle of this educated and well-mannered Creole young lady haphazardly wielding an ax in a torrential rain is too embarrassing to speak of, either because of Léontine's "unseemly" behavior, her pinched financial state, or both. The ax's value to Willet, then, more credibly lies in its symbolic reference to how the two met than in its signification of his bride's self-sufficiency, which, if valued by Willet initially, is completely obliterated by the end of the text.

Even more than "The Wood-Choppers," "Polly" is so thoroughly a conventional romance with a happy ending that it is difficult to read Chopin's sentimentality without also anticipating her sarcasm. But there is no sarcasm in this text, for "Polly's Opportunity," as Chopin's original title reads, turns out to be Polly's chance to stage a face-to-face meeting with George, her betrothed, and hopefully to hear news of when "Ferguson will open up in St. Jo" in person.

Because Polly and George share a long-distance courtship, the significance of Ferguson, George's employer, opening up business in St. Joseph, Missouri, is that George will finally have sufficient income for the two to be married. Chopin's comment on the importance of this event, articulated with as earnest an authorial voice as she ever constructed, is:

> What was *not* going to happen when Ferguson opened up in St. Jo? Polly was going to get a better position; or rather, some one else, named George, was going to get a better position, and incidentally through

George Polly was going to get a position which every well-meaning girl, at some time of her life, looks forward to as the beginning of better things. (*CW* 680)

The fact that Polly McQuade, a recognizably white woman and a sensible, intelligent, and adept assistant bookkeeper for a real estate agency, looks to marriage "to get a better position," indicates just how far afield this text is from Chopin's other, penetrating cultural critiques. Even though "McQuade" is an Irish surname, Chopin does not treat Polly in this text as an ethnic Other who needs to be acculturated to a more pervasive Americanism. Rather, Chopin assumes Polly's identity will be comprehended by her editors and readers as one of the mainstream, and so she is not condoning orthodox feminine ideals here in the name of assimilating Polly into the dominant culture.[24]

Polly's opportunity arises once her Uncle Ben from Fort Worth "has struck it rich in a small way" (*CW* 681) and unexpectedly sends Polly the princely sum of $100 to be spent entirely as she chooses. Polly, the ever-devoted employee, atypically requests the afternoon off work and in the short span of a single afternoon selflessly spends the entire sum on everyone in her family but herself.

Though Polly's abilities as a business woman — her efficiency and her facility with numbers — suggest her well-suitedness for a career outside the home, the only career Chopin has Polly desire is domesticity, and the abilities Polly demonstrates toward that end are those of a resourceful consumer. Ellen Garvey's study of the relationship between fiction and advertising in American magazines between 1880 and 1910 demonstrates how periodicals of the period constructed the female reader as consumer through fiction's representation of women (usually housewives) buying the very items the magazines advertised. Chopin's "Polly" stands as a prime example of this phenomenon, since Polly, the wife-to-be, spends her money primarily on household items, with a particularly keen eye for bargains. Polly purchases a sitting-room lamp at reduced cost as well as some sitting-room curtains that were a "great bargain" (*CW* 681) and splurges on a matching dinner set that had a "dainty but bygone pattern" (*CW* 681) at the greatly reduced price of $15 from the original $25. Thus, days, when he had got a moose and returned, he found the two men stiff and cold and the boy missing."

"The boy missing?" Dawes's pencil was suspended in mid-air.

"Yes, missing; and never a sign. The camp was close by the river, and McDermott figured

due reward, and great reward, shall be given."

The thing had happened. It was all right to Hoockla-Heen that he should go up the hill holding this tall, dark-bearded man by the hand. For he knew he was going to see the woman, fair and soft, the woman whom he often remembered, whose hair was yellow.

POLLY   BY KATE CHOPIN

POLLY particularly disliked to have her mail addressed to the real estate office in which she was employed as assistant bookkeeper. She pushed aside the businesslike letter which confronted her one morning when she had mounted the high stool before her desk.

What Polly did like was to find letters awaiting her at her boarding-house in the evening, when she might, in the privacy of her room, enjoy reading the news from home or from friends scattered over the western hemisphere.

There was one weekly letter to which Polly especially looked forward. She always read it slowly, as she would have eaten ice-cream, making the delight of it last as long as possible. There was in every one of those letters a cheerful reference to something which was going to happen "when Ferguson opens up in St. Jo"; something that made Polly look as bright as a sparrow on a maple branch.

What was *not* going to happen when Ferguson opened up in St. Jo? Polly was going to get a better position; or rather, some one else, named George, was going to get a better position, and incidentally through George Polly was going to get a position which every well-meaning girl, at some time of her life, looks forward to as the beginning of better things.

When the noon hour came Polly laid aside her

opportunity to feel what it's like to spend money for once in your life. Let me know when Ferguson opens up in St. Jo, and this little transaction will be duplicated. How are you getting on? Love to your mother and the girls.

Affectionately, your Uncle Ben.

"Uncle Ben! Dear, dear Uncle Ben!" exclaimed Polly, with subdued emotion. This was an event in her life, and she met it with prompt decision. She had no intention of disregarding her Uncle Ben's conditions. She at once gave the waiter ten cents, which left a balance in her favor of ninety-nine dollars and ninety cents.

She went straight back to the office and asked the junior partner for an afternoon off. It was the first favor she had asked, and while the junior partner realized the indelicacy of refusing it, he was appalled.

"A *whole* afternoon! And so near the end of the month!"

"Yes, please." A most unfeminine Polly thus to keep her own counsel bottled and bubbling up inside her. Most girls would have—but never mind the other girls; this is about Polly.

It did not take her the whole afternoon to spend that hundred dollars. Uncle Ben would have been rather startled at her promptness in following his wishes. She had often lingered before the shop windows, and in imagination had sometimes spent as much as this and even though she keeps books for a real estate office, the job Chopin illustrates Polly as being particularly well suited for is money-manager of the home.

In the spirit of True Womanhood, Polly selflessly forwards these goods to the people for whom they were purchased — her mother and sisters — and there is a great stir among the neighborhood as the items are delivered. Polly's older sister Isabel sees this as an occasion for throwing a party and invites Polly's fiancé, George, as one of the guests. However, once all the gifts are unwrapped for display and approval, Isabel chides Polly for her frivolity in spending all of her fortune on others:

> "Will you tell me, Polly McQuade, if you've taken leave of your senses?" she asked.
>
> "Senses!" echoed Polly, with round eyes.
>
> "Yes, senses! Have you lost them?"
>
> "Well," said Polly, "I felt I'd left something behind, but I was afraid it was my tooth-brush."
>
> "You're so good at figuring," continued Isabel, "will you kindly figure out how many winters you've been wearing that brown jacket?"
>
> Polly stared down, disconcerted, at the brown jacket; then she began to thump her head with her knuckles, exclaiming:
>
> "Stupid! Stupid!"
>
> "Well, it's to be hoped," went on Isabel, "you have supplied yourself with shoes, stockings, underclothes, a suit, hat, gloves — " but by this time Polly had fled to make a bit of toilet for the evening, which was to be given over to sociability. Isabel had invited the guests, and had written a note to George to be of the number. (*CW* 682–83)

As a woman engaged to be married, Polly — usually a sensible soul — is foolish in Isabel's eyes for not supplying herself with a wedding trousseau for her all-important upcoming role as bride. Polly is stung by the rebuke, and her spirits sink lower and lower as the evening wears on and there is no sign of George.

However, as in all good romances, Polly's knight in shining armor finally appears and brings with him the news that "Ferguson's going to open up in St. Jo on the first of January!" (*CW* 683). All the guests understand the significance of this pronouncement, for "Mrs. McQuade went over and kissed her small daughter and George, and the others felt that congratulations were in order" (*CW* 684). Thus, Polly's windfall — her opportunity — was well used in spite of Isabel's admonitions, for Polly's True Womanhood, her generosity toward others, along with her sense for "figuring," orchestrate what amounts to an engagement party, and so Polly is justly rewarded for her conformity to ideals of turn-of-the-century womanhood, signified through her proficiency at the "job of a lifetime": that of wife.

As if such a resolution were not enough to mark Chopin's tale a romance, Chopin tags on this final paragraph and ends her tale thus:

> It was with great regret that Lord & Pellem had to let Polly go a month later. Where could they find another like her? they asked each other. The senior partner, with an original sense of humor, presented her with a wedding gift in the firm's name: a small brass teakettle containing pieces of money aggregating a month's salary. And he sent it with the humorous injunction: "Polly, put the kettle on!" (*CW* 684).

These words, the last of Chopin's to be seen by her reading public, link Chopin with a tradition of women's writing that she personally eschewed and against which she wrote throughout most of her career.[25] We can only guess that a most desperate Chopin, a Chopin who, in her declining years, wished above all else to be remembered for her achievements as a writer, was willing to radically alter her politics in order to reenter the literary scene. Although late-twentieth-century students of Chopin and of feminism will find it hard not to read Polly's "opportunity" as a chance for independence that was lost as opposed to the chance for marriage that was gained, "Polly," like "The Wood-Choppers," offered Chopin the opportunity she wanted most: the chance to reenter the literary marketplace.

Chopin's willingness to so thoroughly abandon her feminist politics in "Polly" and "The Wood-Choppers," her last two stories, demonstrates just how constrained she must have felt by her own subject position as a woman writer in late-nineteenth-century America. A reading, writing, and decision-making Subject, Chopin was herself nonetheless subject to representation through contemporaneous discursive and cultural practices, and she was so throughout her entire life.[26] Although she may have exaggerated in her own mind the limitations of her marketplace at the end of her career, she did not misjudge them at the beginning. Given her unknown status and lack of connections, Chopin would have had little choice but to enter the national literary scene as she did through the *Youth's Companion*. Such an understanding of why she chose to author the type of fiction she did will hopefully contribute to the ongoing discussion of why we continue to read, teach, and value Kate Chopin.

NOTES

INTRODUCTION

1. The *Companion*'s identity and readership are a complicated matter, in no small part because the only extant account of readership demographics is in Cutts's brief introduction to *The Index to The Youth's Companion*. Billed as a juvenile periodical, the *Companion* did see its primary audience as children who were fairly facile readers. Judging by today's literacy standards, the *Companion* wrote generally to between a fourth- and eighth-grade reading level. However, some of the fiction was quite sophisticated, requiring at least a young adult reader. Chopin's stories fall into this category. Younger children who needed to be read to were accommodated by a separate Children's Page. The *Companion*'s marketing strategies also clearly targeted adults, but because of its emphasis on "youth" I refer to the audience generally as "juvenile readers," understanding, of course, that parents, young adults, and children may also have enjoyed the periodical.

2. "Plenary: Borders and Boundaries in the Race for Race," Convention of the Nineteenth-Century American Women Writers Group, Trinity College, Hartford, 1 June 1996.

3. Chopin used the spelling '*Cadian* as opposed to today's standard, *Cajun*. '*Cadian* was a more direct spelling derivation of *Acadian*, the original term signifying those French colonists and their descendants in Acadia (a region in Canada centering on what is now Nova Scotia) who in the eighteenth century fled encroaching British rule, eventually settling in Louisiana to take advantage of the generous land grants available there after the Seven Years' War.

4. Both McCullough (1999) and I (1997, 1998) have metaphorically figured the relationship between Cajuns and Creoles in Chopin's fiction as "cousins," each with specific class associations.

5. Although the issue has generated serious debate that served its purpose at particular points in time, I believe the current political moment no longer requires scholars to distinguish between regional and local color fiction. For a useful rehearsal of the discussion, see McCullough.

1. KATE CHOPIN'S CANONICAL AND MARKET PLACE

1. Partial quote taken from Chopin's *Book News* rejoinder to *The Awakening*. See Seyersted and Toth, eds., *A Kate Chopin Miscellany* 137.

2. See Toth, appendix III, "The Alleged Banning of *The Awakening*," *Kate Chopin* 422–25; and Thomas.

3. Jones, Gunning, Taylor, and McCullough also identify Chopin — a St. Louis native — as a southern writer and detail the Confederate sympathies of her lived experiences.

4. Research on nineteenth-century white bourgeois femininity in general, and southern femininity in particular, is long and well documented. My discussion of southern womanhood and female authorship in the period is indebted to Coultrap-McQuin, Jones, Kaplan (esp. "Edith Wharton's Profession of Authorship" 65–87), Kelley, and Ryan. For excellent recent applications of these concepts, see contributors in Alves and Cane, eds.

5. Benchmark texts in this regard include those by Gilbert and Gubar; Fetterley, *The Resisting Reader;* and Showalter, *A Literature of Their Own.*

6. For a classic discussion of these constructs, see Smith-Rosenberg 224–25 and 245–96.

7. Lundie's and Goodwyn's separate articles each fall into this category.

8. In this approach I am aided immeasurably by Roediger. See also Schocket's excellent use of the new labor history in his reading of *Life in the Iron Mills.*

9. Both McCullough and I (1998) call upon a metaphor of "waves" to reconstruct a history of Chopin scholarship.

10. I refer to *Young Dr. Gosse,* a nonextant manuscript, and *At Fault* as Chopin's first two novels.

11. See *Library of Southern Literature* 863–66; Pattee; *Dictionary of American Biography,* vol. IV, 90–91; and Quinn 354–57.

12. Chopin has duped even today's most scrupulous scholars, allowing such fictions to be handed down about her. Jones, for instance, claimed that Chopin "wrote quickly, once her idea had formed, in a room swarming with children, their friends, and their activities" (139). Jones was possibly extrapolating from a comment Chopin's son Felix made posthumously about his mother; see *Miscellany,* 166–68. As Toth has also noted, by the time Chopin began writing in 1888, her "children," the youngest of whom was nine, were old enough to respect their mother's privacy when she desired it. Also, her handwritten manuscripts in St. Louis display rigorous revision.

13. See Koppleman 801. An incident in Chopin's career bears out such a strategy's efficacy. When William Dean Howells, an editor at *Harper's,* read Chopin's short story "Boulôt and Boulotte" in the magazine's companion juvenile, *Harper's Young People,* he wrote her a personal note encouraging her to produce more pieces like it. Toth writes that the Howells "note no longer exists" (*Kate Chopin* 192). Ironically, Howells never accepted one of Chopin's subsequent manuscripts. See also Seyersted, *Kate Chopin: A Critical Biography* 54.

14. *Wide Awake* published "The Lilies"; *Harper's Young People* published "A Very Fine Fiddle," "Boulôt and Boulotte," "The Bênitouis' Slave," and "A Turkey Hunt"; and the *Youth's Companion* published "For Marse Chouchoute," "A Wizard from Gettysburg," "A Rude Awakening," "Beyond the Bayou," "Loka," "Mamouche," "A Matter of Prejudice," "Polydore," "Aunt Lympy's Interference," "The Wood-Choppers," and "Polly."

15. These figures include ten stories the juvenile periodicals paid for but didn't print. *Harper's Young People* bought but never published "Old Aunt Peggy," as did the *Companion* with "A Red Velvet Coat," "After the Winter," "Madame Martel's Christmas Eve," "Ti Frère," "A Little Country Girl," "Alexandre's Wonderful Experience," "A December Day in Dixie," "The Gentleman from New Orleans," and "Millie's First Party." Figures are calculated from Chopin's Account/Memo books, 1888–1895 and 1888–1902, Kate Chopin papers, Missouri Historical Society, St. Louis.

16. Seyersted, *Complete Works* 717–18, parenthetically noted hereafter as *CW*. All subsequent references to Chopin's fiction are taken from this volume, still the most complete and definitive collection. Page numbers refer to the 1993 edition.

17. Chopin's Account/Memo books, Missouri Historical Society, St. Louis. The *Chap Book* notation is curious. While Chopin notes she submitted "Lilacs" to the *Chap Book* on 16 March 1995, she also scratches a line through that notation.

18. Bonner notes that "Adrienne and Agathe's relationship has romantic overtones." See his entry "Agathe, Sister" in *The Kate Chopin Companion* 4. Toth (*Chopin* 238) and Vanlandingham (162) also discuss "Lilacs," though not in homoerotic terms.

19. See Smith-Rosenberg, "The Female World of Love and Ritual" 53–76.

20. Qtd. in Toth, *Chopin* 280.

21. Chopin's Account/Memo books, Missouri Historical Society, St. Louis.

22. In her Account/Memo books, Chopin documents that *Vogue* paid $204.80 for eighteen of the nineteen stories it accepted and published. Chopin does not record the amount *Vogue* paid for "Two Summers and Two Souls," which it published on 7 August 1895.

23. The following information on the *Youth's Companion* comes from Cutts, "Introduction" v–xvii; Kelly, *Mother Was a Lady* and *Children's Periodicals of the United States*; and Mott, *A History of American Magazines*, vol. II; vol. III; and vol. IV, 262–74.

24. Although some of the pay discrepancy can be explained by story length, even the pay per word seems to vary throughout Chopin's career, perhaps fluctuating with the author's notoriety at a given time, along with other market con-

cerns, such as the magazines' circulations in a particular year. Figures are from Chopin's Account/Memo books, Missouri Historical Society, St. Louis.

25. The *Companion* bought five of Chopin's stories between 1899 and 1900 that it did not publish.

26. Although Cutts writes that the *Companion* had "the largest audience of readers in the world" in the 1890s (xiv), Mott's figures are more reliable. With the exception of mail-order papers, the *Companion* outpaced all other American magazines in 1885 with a circulation of 385,000; it fell behind only *Ladies' Home Journal* and *Comfort* in 1890 with a circulation of 500,000, and it was fourth in line in 1895 with 600,000 subscribers. See Mott, vol. III, 6, and vol. IV, 16–17.

27. Letters of William Henry Rideing to William Morris Colles 1894–1918, Boston Public Library/Rare Books Department. Courtesy of the Trustees.

28. Even young child readers were accommodated with verse, riddles, and short, short stories on a separate Children's Page.

29. Partial quote from Matthew Arnold's "The Function of Criticism at the Present Time," first published in 1864.

30. The same strategy is used today to develop popular, long-running children's television programs, such as *Sesame Street*, with its guest appearances by adult film stars, pop culture celebrities, and current political figures.

31. In vol. II, Mott writes that "many an adult liked the simpler manner which these great adopted for the benefit of the *Companion* readers," 270.

32. *Dictionary of American Biography*, vol. VI (New York: Scribner's, 1931), 513–14.

33. This is Kelly's primary argument in *Mother Was a Lady*.

34. Qtd. in Mott, vol. IV, 215.

35. The account of Ford's life is taken from *Dictionary of American Biography*, vol. VI. No biography or collection of Ford's private papers exists.

36. Qtd. in Mott, vol. IV, 217.

37. The following discussion of the role played by regionalist periodical fiction in general, and southern periodical fiction in particular, in the literary movement of realism is indebted to both Kaplan's and Taylor's studies, as well as Diffley's and Gabler-Hover's essays.

38. See Sandweiss's introduction and the superb essays in her collection, especially those by Trachtenberg and Hales. Hales's scholarship yields the 1866 quote by Edward L. Wilson, "the camera is mightier than the pen" (qtd. in Hales 209).

Nineteenth-century British intellectual Matthew Arnold's essays "The Function of Criticism at the Present Time" and "The Study of Poetry" are also instructive in this vein. Additionally, see Folkerts and Teeter's account of journalism's circuitous path to truth claims, especially 209–304.

39. Prominent independent journalist Ted Gup has very recently argued for the popular imagination to separate "serious journalists'" from "media" due to journalism's "credibility."

40. See particularly Kathleen Diffley's article, "Home from the Theatre of War."

41. Robbins demonstrates that women's authorization to write about the sphere they inhabit can be traced back to earlier in the century.

42. For two more interesting discussions of the politics informing regionalism's aesthetics, especially as they relate to nation building, see Foote and McCullough.

43. Kaplan 11. Though she uses the language of "both" in this quote to suggest that the effacement and reinscription of social hierarchies occur simultaneously in New England local color texts, Kaplan's argument suggests that social hierarchies are reinscribed *through* their effacement. In the effort to assert internal likenesses, Kaplan argues, the erasure of external differences (such as class and gender) actually *produces* the blind spot of material, social, and political inequities.

44. See Sollors, "Ethnicity," *Critical Terms* 288–305; and *The Invention of Ethnicity.*

45. Appiah, "Race," *Critical Terms* 274–87.

46. The state of Louisiana in the 1890s also marks the historical time and place when long-standing erosions of rights conferred by the Fourteenth and Fifteenth Amendments were finally sanctified by law. The Louisiana Constitution set into motion black disenfranchisement by the passage of a "grandfather clause" in 1898, wherein one had to prove either he or one of his ancestors voted back in 1867, a year when blacks were not allowed to vote (Williamson 233); and segregation was deemed constitutional in 1896, when the separate but equal decision was handed down by the U.S. Supreme Court in Louisiana's Plessy vs. Ferguson case.

47. See Fredrickson, and Williamson's (still) definitive *The Crucible of Race.*

48. This quotation is from Marshall, the old black male servant of the retired Creole Doctor John-Luis, as he speaks to the rascally Cajun boy, Mamouche, in Chopin's "Mamouche," *Complete Works* 268.

2. COLORING LOCALS

1. Kate Chopin, "For Marse Chouchoute: A Colored Boy's Fidelity." *Youth's Companion* 64 (20 August 1891): 450–51.

2. The following discussion of the campaign to color Creoles white is summarized from Tregle 131–85.

3. I would myself be perpetuating a fiction if I suggested that the "formerly hegemonic Spanish-and-French populations" descended *purely* from European colonizers. As colonizers, these new rulers engendered children with the Native

Americans, whose land they took, as well as with the Africans whom they imported as slaves. However, when Anglo Americans migrated to the state, the people in power identified themselves according to their European colonialist past, regardless of their "pure" or "mixed" racial heritage, in order to argue for their "prior rights" to continued positions of dominance.

4. For a personal history of Creoles of color who became successful planters, see Mills.

5. Early, otherwise path-breaking Chopin scholars misapprehended Chopin's racial representations, underscoring the need for more historically sensitive readings of her identity constructions. Bonner, for one, confused the racial identities of Chouchoute and Wash:

> Wash, a white boy, undertakes a responsibility to deliver the community mail to the train station in "Marse Chouchoute." . . . Much of the narrative focuses on the black youngster's concern that Wash's failure to meet his responsibilities will have a devastating effect on his life and family. He does not reflect on the danger in which his mission places him, and it appears that his measurement of happiness is directly proportionate and identifiable with that of his white friend. ("Christianity" 119)

6. For a discussion of the origins of these categories, see Domínguez, especially 133–48. Roediger brilliantly details what was at stake in whiteness for poor laborers should blackness not be enslaved (58).

7. Tregle names Louisiana business leaders, politicians, and intellectuals such as Charles Gayarré, Alfred Mercier, Athanase Nicolopolus, and Alcée Fortier as leaders in this movement.

8. Why Chopin sometimes represents Creoles, the supposed descendants of French and Spanish nobility, as indigents in her texts is not self-evident. However, the fatherless and impoverished southern family that fell from a prosperous antebellum past into its current economic state as a result of the war is a staple of postbellum southern fiction. That Chopin's Creole characters are heirs to that grand past can be seen in their use of standard English, their genteel behaviors, and their imitation of conventional gender norms. They are thus the "impoverished gentry," bearers of noble blood without money.

9. Frederickson's and Williamson's studies argue that the construction of "race" as it is currently used originated in the nineteenth century. See also Allen.

10. As with her Kentucky Protestant protagonist Edna Pontellier in *The Awakening*, Chopin's own ethnic affiliation was to be among, but not necessarily one, with Creoles. Because she was born in St. Louis, Missouri, to a mother of Euro-

pean French descent and an Irish immigrant father, she could not lay technical claim to Creole identity. However, her own maternal French heritage, as well as her marriage to Oscar Chopin, a bonafide Louisiana Creole whose mother descended from French immigrants and whose father emigrated from France, aligned her sympathetically with peoples of Gallic ancestry.

11. See Jones, Scott, and Genovese.

12. For more on the mutual construction of violent black male desire and saintly white femininity, see Ware 167–224, and Gunning, *Race*.

13. For an accounting of such texts, see Ryan, *Empire*.

14. See Starke for a study of representations of African Americans in American literature.

15. Tregle explains that the myth of the Creole as a descendant of European nobility parlayed Creolism's repudiation of the American (read: Protestant) work ethic as the "naturally" artistic sensibilities of its people. Instead of sweating by their brow, so the myth went, Creoles were accomplished in the art of appreciating life's finer moments.

16. Gunning's quote regards the character Gregoire in Chopin's first novel, *At Fault* ("Kate Chopin . . . and the Politics of White Supremacy" 70).

17. Kate Chopin, "A Wizard from Gettysburg," *Youth's Companion* 65 (7 July 1892): 346–47.

18. For discussions of the rise of the professions and their importance to the middle class, see Wiebe 111–32; and Trachtenberg, *Incorporation* 140–81.

19. Scott argues this point in her introduction; see also Genovese.

20. Rotundo argues that, while the American Revolution spawned the formation of the defiant American male individual, industrialization in the North and expansionism in the West further encouraged entrepreneurial individualism and rugged individualism, respectively, both regional versions of self-made manhood. See especially 11–25.

21. Rotundo writes of colonial New England and antebellum southern times: "Fathers were expected to advise their sons on [the matter of choosing a career], and they used whatever influence they had to get their young men started," 26–27.

22. Roediger would, of course, disagree. He argues that whiteness paid at the very least psychological, if not material, "wages."

23. The following discussion on the discursive and social histories of Acadian people and their descendants is indebted to Brasseaux, Conrad and the contributors to his collection, Domínguez, Tregle, and the able editors at *Louisiana Literature*, whose comments first shaped this reading.

24. Although Elfenbein misreads the white Calixta ("At the 'Cadian Ball"; "After the Storm") as a mixed-race character, her error nonetheless demonstrates how ethnic whiteness is mitigated by a female body's distance from accepted gender and sexual mores. See McCullough's use of this argument in regard to the American Edna in *The Awakening*.

25. We should not forget that the *Companion* provided an illustration for "A Rude Awakening" that clearly portrays Lolotte as white. The illustration no doubt helped readers correctly apprehend Chopin's lesson on racial identity.

26. As Bederman has argued, for such traditional models of nineteenth-century family relations, manliness was the central ideal of whiteness; to be a "man," by class and gender definitions, was to be white.

27. Chopin's fiction articulates Cajun dialect as distinctive. The substitution of a personal pronoun for an intensive pronoun at the end of an independent clause (as in Lolotte's "'I'm wo' out, me!'") is another way in which Chopin marks Cajun identity.

3. FOR THE LOVE OF CHILDREN

1. Douglas 6; and Smith 15.

2. Ryan, *The Empire of the Mother*.

3. Ryan situates the "empire of the mother" as a midcentury construct that was already on the decline by the time Henry C. Wright's book by the same name came out in 1870. As Ryan's work documents, discourses on imperial motherhood began circulating as early as the 1830s, and Wright's book may simply mark the beginning of the end of that kind of public discussion.

4. For discussions of the nineteenth-century Romantic child as a creature of primal innocence who is close to God and nature and who is both redeemable and redeeming, see Ariès, Calvert, Grylls, MacLeod (*American Childhood*), and Wishy.

5. For a biographical and interpretive account of Rousseau's *Emile*, see Cranston, especially pages 175–83.

6. Only after age twelve did Rousseauesque doctrine advocate introducing rational instruction. As the religiously didactic tradition of early British and American children's literature bears out, eighteenth-century Protestants thought that the earlier rationality was taught to children, the better, since, as essentially depraved creatures in an age of high infant mortality, young folk had precious little time to save their souls.

7. It is important to note that although MacLeod and Grylls both connect the construct of the Romantic child with Rousseau, they differ in those factors to which we can attribute the dominance of such a discursive type. Grylls, a scholar

of British fiction, links the ascendancy of the Romantic child with the rise of British Romanticism and the reification of children as "seers, prophets and guides" (35). MacLeod, an Americanist, makes two claims: (1) that children's fiction was modeling the popular adult sentimental novel in America; and (2) that "sentiment in children's literature was borne in on a wave of social concern for the children of the urban poor," *American Childhood* 146.

8. Carby's work is founded on evidence that documents how, historically, maternal "unfitness" was the main argument used to deny African American females access to "legitimate womanhood." See Gunning's reading of Manna Loulou in "La Belle Zoraïde," *Race* 128–35.

9. For just two accounts of nineteenth-century-women's relationship to the professionalization of medicine and its usurpation of traditional women's roles, see McMillen, and Haller and Haller.

10. See Bonner's first entry, "Loka," in *The Kate Chopin Companion* 92.

11. "Loca" is, of course, the feminine form of the Spanish word for "mad" or "crazy." As a biographical note, Toth writes in *Kate Chopin* (164–72) that Lodoiska DeLouche Sampite, whose nickname was also "Loca," was the wife of Cloutierville planter Albert Sampite, with whom Chopin had extramarital intimacies.

12. Ewell 62; and Toth, *Kate Chopin* 202.

13. See Starke 126; and Harris.

14. Chopin's texts beyond those published in the *Companion* employ sensory-explosive imagery to signal female liberation. In "Story of an Hour," the intoxicating thought of freedom from the responsibilities of Victorian marriage come to Louise Mallard "out of the sky, reaching toward her through the sounds, the scents, the color that filled the air" (*CW* 353). Though the meaning of sensory imagery at the end of *The Awakening* is far more controversial, the last things Edna Pontellier experiences before she drowns are "the hum of bees, and the musky odor of pinks fill[ing] the air" (*CW* 1000).

15. In this way "Mamouche" and "Polydore" differ from the other three stories discussed earlier in the chapter. Rather than represent these two Cajun boys as full-blown Romantic children, Chopin instead draws them as flawed youngsters who nonetheless have a natural capacity for goodness. Her strategy here is not only critical in its attempt to color Mamouche and Polydore white but also important as a persuasive argument aimed at her (imagined) readership to view these boys as different on the surface but essentially the same as themselves.

16. Voorhies notes that one source of this stereotype stemmed from the fact that many Cajun subsistence farmers were forced to take temporary paid labor

jobs following the Civil War because it left their farms ravaged beyond renewal. These farmers, whose former work philosophy was to cultivate only what they and their families needed to survive, understandably balked at working the long, grueling hours demanded by larger plantation owners — often Creoles — who subscribed to the emerging American ideology of materialism. Whereas the Cajuns perceived this (Creole) planter class as greedy, the plantation owners branded the Cajun men as wantonly lazy. Such "facts" gave way to the dominant fiction that Cajun male workers were shiftless, while Creole plantation owners were slave drivers (97–114).

17. The literary type of the bad boy appeared in other texts as well, among them John Haberton's *The Worst Boy in Town* (1880); George Wilbur Peck's *Bad Boy and His Pa* (1883); and Booth Tarkington's *Penrod* (1914) and its two sequels. See *Children's Literature* 238–39.

18. Compare *Wide Awake*'s circulation in 1893 with that of approximately 130,000 for *St. Nicholas* and 500,000 for the *Youth's Companion*.

19. See Bonner's entries "Galopin, Stéphanie"; "John-Luis, Doctor"; "'Mamouche'"; and "Peloté, Théodule," pages 59, 79, 97, and 120, respectively.

20. Tregle claims that literary participation in the discursive campaign to declare Creoles white in the late nineteenth century was set into motion largely by the national popularity of G.W. Cable's *The Grandissimes* (1880), whose portrayal of Louisiana Creoles was anything but sympathetic.

21. The quintessential literary example of the romanticized African American is Harriet Beecher Stowe's Uncle Tom in *Uncle Tom's Cabin*. Chopin replicates Stowe's literary type in the character of Wash in "For Marse Chouchoute."

4. BEYOND COLORING LOCALS

1. Although the stories discussed in this chapter still, inevitably, "color locals" in their representations of characters classified by gender, class, ethnicity, and race, I mean to point out that they concern themselves more with recognizably white characters than they do with characters on the color line. For a sensitive account of how blackness shapes representations of whiteness, even when black characters are absent from a text, see Kenneth Warren.

2. Thomas's response to this question is interesting and useful, though I believe Chopin was disheartened with critiques of *The Awakening*'s morality. See my response to Thomas in "Coloring Locals," diss., 173–81.

3. "A Little Country Girl" was written in February 1899; "A December Day in Dixie" and "Alexandre's Wonderful Experience" in January 1900; and "The Gentleman from New Orleans" in February 1900. *The Awakening* was first published on 22 April 1899.

4. The *Century* had previously published four of Chopin's short stories: "A No-Account Creole" in January 1894; "Azélie" in December 1894; "Regret" in May 1895; and "Ozème's Holiday" in August 1896. It also printed "In Spring," a poem, in July 1899.

5. Herbert S. Stone and Company reneged on its commitment to publish Chopin's third collection of short stories, *A Vocation and a Voice*. See Toth's explanation in *Kate Chopin* (373).

6. Chopin notes in her Account/Memo books that the *Mirror* requested her work. Missouri Historical Society, St. Louis.

7. The two stories Chopin published in the *Mirror* exemplify the kind of female "decadence" that had heretofore been acceptable only to *Vogue*. In "The Godmother," Tante Elodie, a virtuous Creole woman beyond reproach in her community, becomes an accomplice to murder when she helps her beloved godson, Gabriel, cover up his crime; and in "A Vocation and a Voice," Chopin depicts a gypsy woman, Suzima, who is free to work and love as she chooses. Suzima initiates a young orphan boy to sexuality, and her sensual delights persuade him to leave the monastery for her.

8. White claims the year 1920 marks the beginning of the period when the modern novel of adolescence is commonly recognized as a distinctive genre. For two classic discussions of the issue see James Johnson, "The Adolescent Hero: A Trend in Modern Fiction," *Twentieth Century Literature* 5 (April 1959): 3–11; and Tasker W. Witham, *The Adolescent in the American Novel, 1920–1960* (New York: Frederick Ungar, 1964).

9. Winn has also noted the similarities between Chopin's character Charlie and Louisa May Alcott's Jo of *Little Women*.

10. See Gallop and Rose.

11. Gallop appropriates Freudian psychoanalytic discourse to reconstruct the theory of female heterosexual development that is articulated within the female phase of the Oedipal complex — penis envy. As Freud theorizes, the girl child, realizing that she is castrated, desires a penis. This desire for a penis occasions the transfer of the female child's desire for the already-castrated mother onto the father, which, through the institution of the incest taboo, is then eventually transferred to a desire for a male baby. Thus, Gallop articulates female heterosexuality as being a series of transfers or displacements of desire that result in the desire for the (male) other's desire, the desire to be what the father desires her to be.

12. See Butler, *Gender Trouble* and *Bodies That Matter*.

13. Both Gallop and Rose read Freud's account of this seduction as necessarily taking place over and over again throughout the daughter's life. The infinite reinactment of the initial Freudian drama that first makes a female child become a

"girl" — the drama that makes a girl child desire to be what her father wants her to be — is, they argue, what keeps a woman "in check," what continually remakes her passive and subordinate identity as "woman."

14. In a parenthetical remark, Seyersted writes that "a Freudian would call [the affinity between Charlie and her father] a fixation and point to the secret outing of the two where they feel 'like a couple of bees in clover,' and recall Kate Chopin's early loss of all her male relatives" (*A Critical Biography* 183).

15. See Gilbert and Gubar, "The Second Coming of Aphrodite." Schweitzer, however, takes umbrage with Gilbert and Gubar on the following point: She claims that Chopin's ending remains firmly rooted *in* culture, appropriating, as it does, metaphors of maternal power and images of nature's fecundity to imaginatively give birth to a nongendered being. Nonetheless, both arguments articulate Chopin's ending as a utopian vision.

16. Blythe has suggested that, as a manuscript of some fifteen thousand words, "Charlie" may have been rejected for periodical publication because of its length. But even a superficial glance at *Companion* issues in the year 1900 confirms that serial publication was common around that time.

17. Neither is Capitola Black's in E.D.E.N. Southworth's *The Hidden Hand*, although White suggests that the novel was acceptable to Southworth's publishers because its melodramatic conventions rendered it a fantastic tale that was not to be taken seriously.

18. According to Smith-Rosenberg, the "Mannish Lesbian" was the social construct reactionaries substituted for the New Woman in their attempt to undermine newly articulated freedoms for women. (A modern-day analogy would be Rush Limbaugh's coining of the term "femi-Nazi" to replace "feminist.") Smith-Rosenberg writes that "to male physicians, politicians, even modernist writers, the New Woman/Mannish Lesbian symbolized disorder in a world gone mad. To feminists she underscored the irrationality and 'unnaturalness' of a world ordered around male definitions of gender and sexuality" (40–41).

19. Susan Tucker, "Reading and Re-reading: The Scrapbooks of Girls Growing into Women, 1880–1918," Wisconsin State Historical Society, Madison, 10 May 1997. I am indebted to Linda Christian-Smith, respondent to Tucker's paper, for the language of "recording" and "re-coding."

20. The rejection of "Charlie" could not have influenced the production of "The White Eagle" because both took place in May 1900. I believe "Charlie" did, however, affect the marketing of "The White Eagle."

21. As in earlier stories, by this time Chopin could count on Creole ethnicity being read as white. "Polly" similarly takes for granted the whiteness of its main character, a young Irish-American woman. But because of both *The Awakening*'s

critical reception and "Charlie's" rejection, it appears Chopin did not bank on white ethnic differences as a defense against white feminist politics; instead, she rewrote her politics.

22. Though these stories still, inevitably, "color locals" in their representations of characters classified by gender, class, ethnicity, and race, I mean to point out that they concern themselves more with recognizably white, middle-class characters than they do with characters on the color line. For a sensitive account of how blackness shapes representations of whiteness, even when black characters are absent from a text, see Kenneth Warren.

23. Chopin also wrote "Millie's First Party" and "Toots' Nurses" in October 1901, after the *Companion* and the *Century* had rejected "Charlie." The *Companion* paid Chopin $30 for "Millie's First Party" but never printed it. "Toots' Nurses" was rejected first by the *Companion* and then the *Mirror*. Neither manuscript survives.

24. As Ignatiev's and Roediger's studies bear out, the Irish struggle for whiteness was won around midcentury. Also, the *Companion*'s illustration of the character Polly depicts a slender, graceful, respectable, white young lady.

25. Chopin, in her devotion to aesthetic principals of Realism, often expressed her desire to write "life, not art" and thus necessarily worked against the tradition of female romance novelists of midcentury. Chopin is not uncommon for her generation of women writers, who were faced with the difficult task of separating themselves from their foremothers in order to escape the ranks of Hawthorne's "scribbling women."

26. I borrow these lines from Hebert's title to Chapter One: Representing Subjects Subject to Representation, in "Straight Talk: Theorizing Heterosexuality in Feminist Postmodern Fiction," diss., Case Western Reserve U, 1995.

BIBLIOGRAPHY

Alderman, Edwin Anderson, and Joel Chandler Harris, eds. *Library of Southern Literature.* Vol. 2. Atlanta: Martin and Hoyt, 1909. 16 vols.

Allen, Theodore. *The Invention of the White Race.* London: Verso, 1994.

Alves, Susan, and Aleta Feinsod Cane, eds. *The Only Efficient Instrument: American Women Writers and the Periodical.* Iowa City: U of Iowa P, 2001.

Ammons, Elizabeth. *Conflicting Stories: American Women Writers at the Turn into the Twentieth Century.* New York: Oxford UP, 1992.

Appiah, Kwame Anthony. "Race." Lentricchia and McLaughlin 274–87.

Ariès, Philippe. *Centuries of Childhood; A Social History of Family Life.* Trans. Robert Baldick. New York: Knopf, 1962.

Armstrong, Nancy. *Desire and Domestic Fiction: A Political History of the Novel.* New York: Oxford UP, 1987.

Arnold, Matthew. "The Function of Criticism at the Present Time." *Critical Theory since Plato.* Ed. Hazard Adams. New York: Harcourt Brace Jovanovich, 1971. 595.

Bederman, Gail. *Manliness and Civilization: A Cultural History of Gender and Race in the United States, 1880–1917.* Chicago: U of Chicago P, 1995.

Benardete, Jane, and Phyllis Moe, eds. *Companions of Our Youth: Stories by Women for Young People's Magazines, 1865–1900.* New York: Frederick Ungar, 1980.

Birnbaum, Michele. "'Alien Hands': Kate Chopin and the Colonization of Race." *American Literature* 66.2 (1994): 301–23.

Bleser, Carol, ed. *In Joy and in Sorrow: Women, Family, and Marriage in the Victorian South, 1830–1900.* New York: Oxford UP, 1991.

Blythe, Anne M. "Kate Chopin's 'Charlie.'" Boren and Davis 207–15.

Bonner, Thomas Jr. "Christianity and Catholicism in the Fiction of Kate Chopin." *Southern Quarterly* 20.2 (Winter 1982): 118–25.

———. *The Kate Chopin Companion, with Chopin's Translations from French Fiction.* Westport: Greenwood, 1988.

Boren, Lynda S., and Sara deSaussure Davis, eds. *Kate Chopin Reconsidered: Beyond the Bayou.* Baton Rouge: Louisiana State UP, 1992.

Brasseaux, Carl A. *Acadian to Cajun: Transformation of a People, 1803–1877.* Jackson: UP of Mississippi, 1992.

Briggs, Julia, and Dennis Butts. "The Emergence of Form (1850–1890)." Hunt 130–66.

Butler, Judith. *Bodies That Matter: On the Discursive Limits of Sex*. New York: Routledge, 1993.

————. *Gender Trouble: Feminism and the Subversion of Identity*. New York: Routledge, 1990.

Calvert, Karin Lee Fishbeck. *Children in the House: The Material Culture of Early Childhood, 1600–1900*. Boston: Northeastern UP, 1992.

Carby, Hazel. *Reconstructing Womanhood: The Emergence of the Afro-American Woman Novelist*. New York: Oxford UP, 1987.

"Children's Literature in America (1870–1945)." Hunt 225–51.

Chopin, Kate. Account/Memo Books, 1888–1895 and 1888–1902. Kate Chopin papers. Missouri Historical Society, St. Louis.

"Chopin, Kate." *Dictionary of American Biography*. Vol. 4. New York: Scribner's, 1930.

Cogan, Frances B. *All-American Girl: The Ideal of Real Womanhood in Mid-Nineteenth-Century America*. Athens: U of Georgia P, 1989.

Conrad, Glenn R., ed. *The Cajuns: Essays on Their History and Culture*. Layfayette: U of Southwestern Louisiana Center for Louisiana Studies, 1978.

Coultrap-McQuin, Susan. *Doing Literary Business: American Women Writers in the Nineteenth Century*. Chapel Hill: U of North Carolina P, 1990.

Cranston, Maurice. *The Noble Savage: Jean-Jacques Rousseau 1754–1762*. Chicago: U of Chicago P, 1991.

Cutts, Richard. Introduction. *Index to the Youth's Companion 1871–1929*. Metuchen, NJ: Scarecrow, 1972. v-xvii.

Cyganowski, Carol Klimick. *Magazine Editors and Professional Authors in Nineteenth-Century America: The Genteel Tradition and the American Dream*. New York: Garland, 1988.

Dictionary of American Biography. Ed. Allen Johnson and Dumas Malone. New York: Scribner's, 1930.

Diffley, Kathleen. "Home from the Theatre of War: The Southern Magazine and Recollections of the Civil War." Price and Smith 183–201.

Dixon, Thomas. *The Leopard's Spots: A Romance of the White Man's Burden — 1865–1900*. [1902] Ridgewood, NJ: Gregg, 1967.

Domínguez, Virginia R. *White by Definition: Social Classification in Creole Louisiana*. New Brunswick: Rutgers UP, 1986.

Donovan, Josephine. *New England Local Color Literature: A Women's Tradition*. New York: Ungar, 1983.

Douglas, Ann. *The Feminization of American Culture*. New York: Avon, 1977.

Elfenbein, Anna Shannon. *Women on the Color Line: Evolving Stereotypes and the Writings of George Washington Cable, Grace King, Kate Chopin.* Charlottesville: UP of Virginia, 1989.

Ewell, Barbara C. *Kate Chopin.* New York: Ungar, 1986.

Fetterley, Judith. *The Resisting Reader: A Feminist Approach to American Fiction.* Bloomington: Indiana UP, 1978.

———, and Marjorie Pryse, eds. *American Women Regionalists 1850–1910: A Norton Anthology.* New York: Norton, 1992.

Fiedler, Leslie A. *Love and Death in the American Novel.* New York: Criterion, 1960.

Fishkin, Shelley Fisher. "Interrogating 'Whiteness,' Complicating 'Blackness': Remapping American Culture." *American Quarterly* 47.3 (September 1995): 428–66.

Folkerts, Jean, and Dwight L. Teeter Jr. *Voices of a Nation: A History of Mass Media in the United States.* 3rd ed. Boston: Allyn and Bacon. 1998.

Foote, Stephanie. *Regional Fictions: Culture and Identity in Nineteenth-Century American Literature.* Madison: U of Wisconsin P, 2001.

"Ford, Daniel Sharp." *Dictionary of American Biography.* Vol. 6. New York: Scribner's, 1931.

Fredrickson, George M. *The Black Image in the White Mind: The Debate on Afro-American Character and Destiny, 1817–1914.* New York: Harper, 1971.

Gabler-Hover, Janet. "The North-South Reconciliation Theme and the 'Shadow of the Negro.' In *Century Illustrated Magazine.*" Price and Smith 239–56.

Gallop, Jane. *The Daughter's Seduction: Feminism and Psychoanalysis.* Ithaca: Cornell UP, 1982.

Gannon, Susan R. "'The Best Magazine for Children of All Ages': Cross-Editing *St. Nicholas Magazine* (1873–1905)." *Children's Literature* 25 (1997): 153–80.

Garvey, Ellen Gruber. *The Adman in the Parlor: Magazines and the Gendering of Consumer Culture.* Oxford: Oxford UP, 1996.

Genovese, Eugene. "'Our Family, White and Black: Family and Household in the Southern Slaveholders' World View." Bleser 69–87.

Gilbert, Sandra M., and Susan Gubar. *The Madwoman in the Attic: The Woman Writer and the Nineteenth-Century Literary Imagination.* 3 vols. New Haven: Yale UP, 1979.

———, eds. *The Norton Anthology of Literature by Women: The Tradition in English.* New York: Norton, 1985.

———. "The Second Coming of Aphrodite: Kate Chopin's Fantasy of Desire." *No Man's Land: The Place of the Woman Writer in the Twentieth Century.* Vol. 2. New Haven: Yale UP, 1988. 83–119.

Gilman, Sander. *The Jew's Body*. New York: Routledge, 1991.

Goodwyn, Janet. "'Dah you is, settin' down lookin' jis' like w'ite folks!':
Ethnicity Enacted in Kate Chopin's Short Fiction." *The Yearbook of English
Studies* 24. London: W. S. Maney and Son, 1994. 1–11.

Grady, Henry W. *The New South*. New York: Robert Bonner, 1890.

———. *The Race Problem*. Philadelphia: John D. Morris, 1900.

Grylls, David. *Guardians and Angels: Parents and Children in Nineteenth-Century
Literature*. Boston: Faber and Faber, 1978.

Gunning, Sandra. "Kate Chopin's Local Color Fiction and the Politics of White
Supremacy." *Arizona Quarterly* 51.3 (Autumn 1995): 61–86.

———. *Race, Rape, and Lynching: The Red Record of American Literature 1890–
1912*. Oxford: Oxford UP, 1996.

Gup, Ted. "'Media' Means So Much, It Means Nothing." *The Chronicle of
Higher Education*. Section 2. *The Chronicle Review* 23 Nov. 2001: B20.

Habegger, Alfred. *Gender, Fantasy and Realism in American Literature*. New
York: Columbia UP, 1982.

Hales, Peter Bacon. "American Views and the Romance of Modernization."
Sandweiss 204–57.

Haller, John S., and Robin M. Haller. *The Physician and Sexuality in Victorian
America*. Urbana: U of Illinois P, 1974.

Hanson, David C., ed. *Louisiana Literature, Special Section Kate Chopin*. 11.1
(Spring 1994).

Harris, Susan K. *Nineteenth-Century American Women's Novels: Interpretive
Strategies*. Cambridge: Cambridge UP, 1990.

Harris, Trudier. *From Mammies to Militants: Domestics in Black American
Literature*. Philadelphia: Temple UP, 1982.

Hawks, Joanne V., and Sheila L. Skemp, eds. *Sex, Race, and the Role of Women in
the South*. Jackson: UP of Mississippi, 1983.

Hebert, Ann Marie. Chapter One: Representing Subjects Subject to
Representation. "Straight Talk: Theorizing Heterosexuality in Feminist
Postmodern Fiction." Diss. Case Western Reserve U, 1995.

Hirsch, Arnold R., and Joseph Logsdon, eds. *Creole New Orleans: Race and
Americanization*. Baton Rouge: Louisiana State UP, 1992.

Huf, Linda. *A Portrait of the Artist as a Young Woman: The Writer as Heroine in
American Literature*. New York: Ungar, 1983.

Hunt, Peter, ed. *Children's Literature: An Illustrated History*. Oxford: Oxford UP,
1995.

Ignatiev, Noel. *How the Irish Became White*. New York: Routledge, 1995.

Johnson, James. "The Adolescent Hero: A Trend in Modern Fiction." *Twentieth Century Literature* 5 (April 1959): 3–11.

Jones, Anne Goodwyn. *Tomorrow Is Another Day: The Woman Writer in the South, 1859–1936*. Baton Rouge: Louisiana State UP, 1981.

Kaplan, Amy. *The Social Construction of American Realism*. Chicago: U of Chicago P, 1988.

Kelley, Mary. *Private Woman, Public Stage: Literary Domesticity in Nineteenth-Century America*. New York: Oxford UP, 1984.

Kelly, R. Gordon, ed. *Children's Periodicals of the United States*. Westport: Greenwood, 1984.

———. *Mother Was a Lady: Self and Society in Selected American Children's Periodicals 1865–1890*. Westport: Greenwood, 1974.

Koloski, Bernard. *Approaches to Teaching Chopin's "The Awakening."* New York: MLA, 1988.

Koppelman, Susan. "Short Story." *The Oxford Companion to Women's Writing in the United States*. Ed. Cathy N. Davidson and Linda Wagner-Martin. Oxford: Oxford UP, 1995. 798–803.

Lanson, Gerald, and Mitchell Stephens. *Writing and Reporting the News*. 2nd ed. New York: Harcourt Brace College Publishers, 1994.

Lentricchia, Frank, and Thomas McLaughlin, eds. *Critical Terms for Literary Study*. Chicago: U of Chicago P, 1990.

Library of Southern Literature. Vol. II. Atlanta: Martin and Hoyt, 1909.

Lundie, Catherine. "Doubly Dispossessed: Kate Chopin's Women of Color." Hanson 126–44.

MacLeod, Anne Scott. *American Childhood: Essays on Children's Literature of the Nineteenth and Twentieth Centuries*. Athens: U of Georgia P, 1994.

———. "Children's Literature in America from the Puritan Beginnings to 1870." Hunt 102–29.

Martin, Wendy. *New Essays on "The Awakening."* Cambridge: Cambridge UP, 1988.

McCullough, Kate. *Regions of Identity: The Construction of America in Women's Fiction, 1885–1914*. Stanford: Stanford UP, 1999.

McMillen, Sally G. *Motherhood in the Old South: Pregnancy, Childbirth, and Infant Rearing*. Baton Rouge: Louisiana State UP, 1990.

Mills, Gary B. *The Forgotten People: Cane River's Creoles of Color*. Baton Rouge: Louisiana State UP, 1977.

Mott, Frank Luther. *A History of American Magazines*. 5 vols. Cambridge: Harvard UP, 1938–1968.

Patmore, Coventry. "The Angel in the House." Gilbert and Gubar 168.

Pattee, Fred Lewis. *A History of American Literature since 1870.* New York: Century, 1915.

Peel, Ellen. "Semiotic Subversion in 'Désirée's Baby.'" *American Literature* 62.2 (June 1990): 223–37.

Perspectives on Kate Chopin: Proceedings of the Kate Chopin International Conference. Natchitoches: Northwestern State UP, 1990.

"Plenary: Borders and Boundaries in the Race for Race," Convention of the Nineteenth-Century American Women Writers Group, Trinity College, Hartford, 1 June 1996.

Price, Kenneth M., and Susan Belasco Smith, eds. *Periodical Literature in Nineteenth-Century America.* Charlottesville: UP of Virginia, 1995.

Quinn, Arthur Hobson. *American Fiction: An Historical and Critical Survey.* New York: D. Appleton-Century, 1936.

Rankin, Daniel S. *Kate Chopin and Her Creole Stories.* Philadelphia: U of Pennsylvania P, 1932.

Rideing, William Henry. Letters to William Morris Colles, 1894–1918. Ms. Am.144. Rare Books and Manuscripts Room, Boston Public Library.

Robbins, Sarah. "Gendering Gilded Age Periodical Professionalism: Reading Harriet Beecher Stowe's *Hearth and Home* Prescriptions for Women's Writing." Alves and Cane 45–65.

Roediger, David R. *The Wages of Whiteness: Race and the Making of the American Working Class.* New York: Verso. Revised edition. 1999.

Rose, Jacqueline. "Femininity and Its Discontents." *Sexuality in the Field of Vision.* London: Verso, 1986. 83–103.

Rotundo, E. Anthony. *American Manhood: Transformations in Masculinity from the Revolution to the Modern Era.* New York: Basic Books, 1993.

Rousseau, Jean-Jacques. *Emile.* [1762] Trans. Barbara Foxley. New York: Dutton, 1955.

Ryan, Mary P. *The Empire of the Mother: American Writing about Domesticity, 1830–1860.* New York: Institute for Research in History and Haworth, 1982.

———. *Women in Public: Between Banners and Ballots, 1825–1880.* Baltimore: Johns Hopkins UP, 1990.

Sandweiss, Martha, ed. *Photography in Nineteenth-Century America.* New York: Harry N. Abrams, 1991.

Schocket, Eric. "'Discovering Some New Race': Rebecca Harding Davis's *Life in the Iron Mills* and the Literary Emergence of Working-Class Whiteness." *PMLA* 115 (Jaury 2000): 46–59.

Schweitzer, Ivy. "Maternal Discourse and the Romance of Self-Possession in Kate Chopin's *The Awakening*." *Boundary 2: An International Journal of Literature and Culture* 17.1 (Spring 1990): 159–86.

Scott, Anne Furor. *The Southern Lady: From Pedestal to Politics 1830–1930*. Chicago: U of Chicago P, 1970.

Seyersted, Per, ed. *The Complete Works of Kate Chopin*. Baton Rouge: Louisiana State UP, 1969, rpt. 1993.

———. *Kate Chopin: A Critical Biography*. Baton Rouge: Louisiana State UP, 1969.

———, and Emily Toth, eds. *A Kate Chopin Miscellany*. Natchitoches: Northwestern State UP, 1979.

Shaker, Bonnie James. "Coloring Locals: Identity Politics in Kate Chopin's *Youth's Companion* Stories, 1891–1902." Diss. Case Western Reserve U, 1998.

———. "Kate Chopin and the Birth of Young Adult Fiction." *Defining Print Culture for Youth*. Ed. Anne Lundin. Forthcoming, Greenwood.

———. "Kate Chopin and the Periodical: Revisiting the Re-Vision." Alves and Cane 78–91.

———. "'Lookin' Jis' like W'ite Folks': Coloring Locals in Kate Chopin's 'A Rude Awakening.'" *Louisiana Literature* 14.2 (Fall 1997): 116–25.

Showalter, Elaine. *A Literature of Their Own: British Women Novelists from Brontë to Lessing*. Princeton: Princeton UP, 1977.

———. *Sister's Choice: Tradition and Change in American Women's Writing*. New York: Oxford UP, 1991.

Skaggs, Merrill Maguire. *The Folk of Southern Fiction*. Athens: U of Georgia P, 1972.

Skaggs, Peggy. *Kate Chopin*. Boston: Twayne, 1985.

Smith, Stephanie A. *Conceived by Liberty: Maternal Figures and Nineteenth-Century American Literature*. Ithaca: Cornell UP, 1994.

Smith-Rosenberg, Carroll. *Disorderly Conduct: Visions of Gender in Victorian America*. New York: Oxford UP, 1985.

Sollors, Werner. "Ethnicity." Lentricchia and McLaughlin 288–305.

———, ed. *The Invention of Ethnicity*. Oxford: Oxford UP, 1989.

Solomon, Barbara H. Introduction. *The Awakening and Selected Stories of Kate Chopin*. New York: New American Library, 1976.

Starke, Catherine Juanita. *Black Portraiture in American Fiction: Stock Characters, Archetypes, and Individuals*. New York: Basic Books, 1971.

Taylor, Helen. *Gender, Race, and Region in the Writings of Grace King, Ruth McEnery Stuart, and Kate Chopin*. Baton Rouge: Louisiana State UP, 1989.

Thomas, Heather Kirk. "'What Are the Prospects for the Book?': Rewriting a Woman's Life." Boren and Davis 36–60.

Toth, Emily. Introduction. Hanson 8–17.

———. *Kate Chopin*. Austin: U of Texas P, 1990.

———, ed. *Regionalism and the Female Imagination: A Collection of Essays*. New York: Human Sciences, 1985.

Trachtenberg, Alan. *The Incorporation of America: Culture and Society in the Gilded Age*. New York: Hill and Wang, 1982.

———. "Photography: The Emergence of a Keyword." Sandweiss 16–47.

Tregle, Joseph Jr. "Creoles and Americans." Hirsch and Logsdon 131–88.

Tucker, Susan. "Reading and Re-reading: The Scrapbooks of Girls Growing into Women, 1880–1918." Wisconsin State Historical Society, Madison. 10 May 1997.

Vanlandingham, Phyllis. *Perspectives on Kate Chopin*. 159–67.

Voorhies, Jacqueline. "The Acadians: The Search for the Promised Land." Conrad 97–114.

Ware, Vron. *Beyond the Pale: White Women, Racism and History*. London: Verso, 1992.

Warren, Joyce W., ed. *The (Other) American Traditions: Nineteenth-Century Women Writers*. New Jersey: Rutgers UP, 1993.

Warren, Kenneth. *Black and White Strangers: Race and American Literary Realism*. Chicago: U of Chicago P, 1993.

White, Barbara A. *Growing Up Female: Adolescent Girlhood in American Fiction*. Westport: Greenwood, 1985.

Wiebe, Robert. *The Search for Order, 1877–1920*. New York: Hill and Wang, 1967.

Williamson, Joel. *The Crucible of Race: Black-White Relations in the American South since Emancipation*. Oxford: Oxford UP, 1984.

Winn, Harbor. "Echoes of Literary Sisterhood: Louisa May Alcott and Kate Chopin." *Studies in American Fiction* 20.2 (Autumn 1992): 205–8.

Wishy, Bernard W. *The Child and the Republic: The Dawn of Modern American Child Nurture*. Philadelphia: U of Pennsylvania P, 1968.

Witham, Tasker W. *The Adolescent in the American Novel, 1920–1960*. New York: Frederick Ungar, 1964.

INDEX

Page numbers in *italics* refer to illustrations. Story and book titles not otherwise identified were authored by Chopin.

34, 90. *See also* gender norms;
women and womanhood
Seyersted, Per, 1, 92, 109, 115, 136n14
Sheehan, Donald, 19
short stories, xii, 5–6
"A Singular Class of Men," 7–8, 10
Sister Agathe (character), 10
Skaggs, Peggy, 2
Smith, Stephanie, 57
Smith-Rosenberg, Carroll, 136n17
social order. *See* class; families and
family values; men and manhood;
religion; women and womanhood
Sollors, Werner, 25
South, influence on Chopin, 1
Southworth, E.D.E.N., 99, 136n17
Spanish population of Louisiana,
28–29
St. Louis Criterion, 7
St. Louis Post-Dispatch, 1
St. Nicholas, 16, 134n18
Stanley, Henry M., 15
Starke, Catherine Juanita, 72
Stéphanie Galopin (character), 78, 80–
81, 83–84
stereotypes, 36, 65, 77, 80, 82–83,
133n16
Stoltz, Paula von, 115
"The Storm," 8
The Story of a Bad Boy (Aldrich), 78
"Story of an Hour," 133n14
Stowe, Harriet Beecher, 15, 30, 134n21
Stuart, Ruth McEnery, 95
subversion: in "Charlie" character,
109; femininity and, 59; masking
as, 2; in "Polly," 114–15; in "Wood-
Choppers," 114–15, 118
Sylveste Bordon (character), 47, 49–
50, 55

Taylor, Helen, 4, 23–24
Tennyson, Alfred Lord, 15
Théodule Peloté (character), 80–81,
83, 86
"Three Portraits," 10
"Ti Démon," 99
"Ti Frère," 127n15
Tontine (character), 66–67, 68, 70
"Toots' Nurses," 137n23
Toth, Emily: on "Beyond the Bayou,"
71; on Chopin's racial politics, 3–5;
on "Lilacs," 127n18; on note from
Howells, 126n13; on relationship
with Reedy, 97; on subversion, 2;
on "Ti Démon," 99; on unpub-
lished stories, 94; on writing prac-
tices, 126n12
Tregle, Joseph, 28–29, 134n20
True Womanhood: maternity requisite
for, 60; in "Polly," 121, 122; vs. Real
Womanhood, 108; Romantic child,
57, 59; in "The Wood-Choppers,"
115; Woman Question, 2
Tucker, Susan, 109
Twain, Mark, 78
"Two Summers and Two Souls," 11,
127n22

Uncle Ben (character), 119
Uncle Gervais (character), 112
Uncle Tom's Cabin (Stowe), 30, 134n21
"The Unexpected," 11

Vanlandingham, Phyllis, 7–9, 10,
127n18
Victor Annibelle (character), 113
violence, 21, 26, 33–34, 65, 71
"A Visit to Avoyelles," 11
"A Vocation and a Voice," 97, 135n7